D0291129

GOD SPOKE, NOW WHAT?

Activating Your Prophetic Word

DOUG ADDISON

Printed in USA by InLight Connection
PO Box 7049, Santa Maria, CA 93456

For ordering information contact: InLight Connection (800) 507-7853
To order: DougAddison.com

Cover Design by Christian Wetzel

Book design by Treasure Image & Publishing
TreasureImagePublishing.com (248) 403-8046

CONTENTS

INTRODUCTION

I am so excited that you are taking a step towards developing your ability to hear God. If you picked up this book, then chances are that at some point in your life you have heard the voice of God, received a prophetic word and wondered what to do with it. Whether you got a prophetic word from me, someone else, or if God spoke to you directly, this book will help because it contains practical ways to help you respond to what God has given to you. Too often people will get a prophetic word from God but they do not follow through with it, let alone activate it in their lives. I am excited to share some principles and practices that will really help you.

My prayer for you is that God will open your spiritual eyes and ears so that you can understand what He is saying to you, and why He is saying it. I want you to know how to get into God's timing so you can understand what is for now and what is for later. Whether you are praying through small or large amounts of revelation, my goal for you is that it would expand into great things for the Kingdom of God.

My First Encounter With Prophecy

It was 1988 and I went to my sister's church because a minister was there who had the gift of prophecy. He said to my brother-in-law, "You need to lose weight." I was thinking that it was not all that prophetic (maybe it was discernment of the obvious) because he was quite heavy. Then he said to me, "The woman you are with is not the one." Hmmm ... I was with a woman and was going to get married even though my friends and family did not agree.

I thought getting married to the woman I was with at the time was the right thing for me to do. We had been together for seven years and I had come back to God in the process. She was not in the same place as me spiritually and like many people, I really wanted to be married. Then a year later the woman I married left me, and my brother-in-law died of a heart attack! Wow! God got my attention with prophecy.

I went through a painful season of my life with a divorce that could have been avoided had I understood what God was saying to me and responded appropriately. I am now remarried to an amazing woman, Linda, and we have been together for twenty years. And yes, it was the result of hearing God's voice and responding.

God got my attention and I set out on a journey to learn more about this gift of prophecy and how it works. It has been a lifelong process of learning to hear God's voice. I have now dedicated my life and ministry to helping people hear God for their life situations. What I will be sharing with you in this book can save you time and possibly a lot of pain.

You can actually accelerate your process by learning from someone else who has mastered their gifts. Since 1991 I have studied, journaled, written books, ran study groups and even mentored with some amazing prophetic people. I traveled and ministered with Prophets Bob Jones, Larry Randolph and John Paul Jackson to name a few.

In 2001, my wife and I sold all that we owned and launched our ministry, *InLight Connection*. We train people to hear God's voice through developing their prophetic gifts. We also train people to understand how God speaks through the dreams we have at night. I discovered that many night dreams reveal our life dreams, so I am also a life coach and have helped thousands of people to activate what God is saying to them.

The Purpose Of Activation

God speaks in so many ways, yet most people miss it. One thing that Jesus often taught through the parables is that in the Kingdom of God we must have *eyes that see* and *ears that hear*. (Matthew 13:16) He was talking about seeing and hearing spiritual things so that we may come to know His voice. God truly is speaking all the time, but most people are either missing or not understanding what is being said to them.

I base everything I do on Ephesians 1:17, *"I keep asking that the God of our Lord Jesus Christ, the glorious Father, may give you the Spirit of wisdom and revelation, so that you may know him better."*

The sole purpose of hearing God and the reason I wrote this book is so that you may know Him better! It is not to get a wild prophetic word; it truly is about knowing God better.

"I pray that the eyes of your heart may be enlightened in order that you may know the hope to

which he has called you, the riches of his glorious inheritance in his holy people, and his incomparably great power for us who believe." Ephesians 1:18–19a

The closer we get to God, the clearer His voice becomes. The apostle Paul compares God's wisdom and revelation to riches. These are the true riches that God wants to open up to you, namely, the ability to hear His voice. It is amazing.

"But the one who prophesies speaks to people for their strengthening, encouraging and comfort." 1 Corinthians 14:3

I base hearing God and the gift of prophecy on this Bible verse. This is what we are aiming for. When we hear the Father's voice and begin to offer words to others, the goal is that they would be strengthened, encouraged and comforted. There are unfortunately many examples of prophetic words that consist mainly of judgment or other negative things.

This is because they come through people with a filter and belief system that God speaks in an Old Testament way. I believe that prophecy should result in strengthening, encouragement and comfort.

9

Yes, God can speak words of direction and even correction, but when delivering these words, you need to do so with tactfulness and wisdom. Since many people have a negative view of God the Father, communicating more negativity might not bring about the change in the person's life God intended. God is calling you to go beyond just hearing His voice and take it a step further to understand the love of God for them and help change their lives.

HEARING GOD CAN CHANGE YOUR LIFE

As we talk about hearing God, so many different things might go through your mind. Most people think that you have to be a prophet or have a prophetic gift to hear God. Yes, some people are gifted by God to hear Him more clearly than others. I am convinced that we all can hear God, and that God wants us to hear His voice.

Hearing God does not need to be mystical. I like to think of the supernatural things of God as being a natural part of our lives. That would make us naturally supernatural. You do not have to be a prophet to hear the voice of God. As we develop this ability, it will help us to get into our destiny much more quickly if we are able to hear God guiding us. It is also beneficial to us in developing a deeper relationship with God.

There are literally countless benefits to hearing God, including breaking the power of fear in our lives, gaining insight, growing in our faith, and healing. It is important that we understand clearly what God is saying to us. Misunderstanding or misinterpreting what God has said has caused disappointment and even heartbreak in some. Some people have even given up trying to hear God. Sometimes I find that people let go of hearing God, and they end up feeling disconnected from His love. But when we invite them to come back to hearing God, they discover that there are so many benefits. It is amazing to see them reconnect and start to know Him better. In fact, their fears are broken off and healing happens.

One benefit of hearing God is that it breaks the power of fear over us. Did you know that discernment allows you to have perfect peace? It brings healing. In Luke 6:18, it says that people from everywhere came to hear Jesus and they were healed. There is an amazing connection between hearing and healing. Healing does not have to be physical only. There is also emotional, relational and spiritual healing that happens.

Hearing God's voice not only brings healing, but also healing strategies. I will talk later about how God gave me breakthrough and healing strategies that I still use to encourage others. God can bring clear direction to you. John 10:27 says, *"My sheep hear my voice … and they follow me."* (KJV)

It is not just hearing a prophetic word, but hearing God's voice and responding to it that is needed.

Our Faith Increases

"Now faith is being sure of what we hope for, being convinced of what we do not see." Hebrews 11:1 NET

When we are able to hear God clearly, our faith increases. Hearing God helps sustain us in our walk with Him. Not only that, but the apostle Paul teaches that: *"... faith comes from hearing the message, and the message is heard through the word about Christ."* Romans 10:17

It is interesting how some people believe that all we need is the Bible. I believe we need the Bible, but we also need the Holy Spirit to instruct us on how to apply what is in the Bible. We need God's written Word, His spoken prophetic word and guidance through the Holy Spirit which brings it all together in balance.

"In the last days, God says, I will pour out my Spirit on all people. Your sons and daughters will prophesy, your young men will see visions, your old men will dream dreams." Acts 2:17

We are living in a time when we really do need to hear the voice of God. God is truly speaking all the time, but most people have not been trained on how to understand or discern what is being spoken to them. There have been some bad examples and misuse of the prophetic gifts. But just because someone has not used the gift correctly or wounded others does not mean we should stop listening to God. An amazing world will open to you when you do!

Fear Of Being Deceived

"But solid food is for the mature, who by constant use have trained themselves to distinguish good from evil." Hebrews 5:14

Many people are afraid of being deceived when it comes to hearing God. According to Hebrews 5:14, the remedy for this is to train yourself, which will take practice. One reason why many people do not hear God consistently is because they have not practiced listening and activating what they are hearing. They may also have trouble discerning whether what they hear is from God, themselves, or other sources. Practice is required to grow and mature in our spiritual life.

Here is a practical example of what I am talking about. People who work with money in the banking industry must be able to distinguish between real and counterfeit money. To be able to tell the difference between the two, you would need to become very familiar with real money to the point that you sensitized yourself to recognizing it right off the bat. Then, if you came across counterfeit money, you would immediately be able to recognize "the fake" just by touch or by sight, because you have become so sensitive to "the real" through practice.

These same principles apply to hearing God and receiving a prophetic word. We must learn to be sensitive to the differences between God's voice, our own ideas, and those of demonic forces. The easiest way to do this is to study your own experiences. Let's say you hear God and there is clear evidence to confirm that what you heard was really God speaking to you. This might be something like an answered prayer or a situation that takes place of which you had no previous knowledge.

Use a journal to record and study what it felt like to hear Him. Remember how it came to you, the sense you had in your spirit, and the peace you had. This is a good and practical way to learn to discern God's voice.

Why God Does Not Always Make It Clear

People often say: "If God wants to speak to me, He will speak to me plainly." Those who are saying this obviously are not familiar with all the different and creative ways that God spoke in the Bible. Jesus did not even speak plainly to His own disciples. The Bible is full of metaphors, symbolism and hidden language. Even just reading the Bible requires some degree of interpretation.

God often conceals things so that those who are hungry and want to know more will search it out. (Proverbs 25:2) God will also hide things from people who consider themselves wise in their own eyes and reveal deep spiritual truths to those who are humble and childlike. (Matthew 11:25–26)

Sometimes God speaks more clearly, but most of the time God speaks to us personally in the form of a small, quiet voice inside of us. Unless we train ourselves to listen to it, then it could be considered a coincidence. Everyone has experienced this at some time in their life. The way spiritual gifts work is that some people have the ability to hear more clearly from God than others. It does not make them more spiritual or mean that God likes them more than those who do not hear God quite as clearly.

Practical Steps To Hearing God

Be expectant that God really does want to communicate with you. Most of the time, we simply need to clear away some of the busyness in our lives to perceive what He is saying.

He longs to convey messages of love, comfort, wisdom, guidance and warnings in a variety of ways. Maybe it is through dreams and visions, the Bible, a conversation we have with someone or by way of nature, music or the arts. The possibilities are endless.

In this book we are talking about how to activate what you are already hearing from God. Sometimes that will be through a prophetic word directly from God or from another person. Hearing God requires us to develop a lifestyle of listening spiritually. The best way is to find time to quiet yourself and listen for His voice.

It helps to find a specific time that you can listen for God to speak each day. It really helps to have peace in your life if you want to hear the voice of God. When you are hurried or stressed out, you are less likely to consistently hear Him. It is good to set time aside regularly, daily if possible, to quiet yourself.

Many of us have busy lives with lots to do, but we do not have to be hurried. You will go through times when you have more or less time with God, depending on your life situation. A key is to think in terms of having a relationship with a living person. God longs for us to spend time with Him like a father would with his children.

I will talk a lot about the fact that we need to take time to journal and write down how God may be speaking to you. I cannot stress the point enough that journaling will change your life beyond what you may believe possible. Quite often God speaks over time and most people miss this process because they do not track it. Since I take time to journal every day, I am continually surprised to see things come to pass that God had spoken to me. In my opinion, hearing God clearly cannot be done without valuing what He is speaking to you and tracking it over time.

The Definition Of False Prophecy

There are many positive benefits of hearing God, but I want to address something right away when it comes to hearing God. Many people have misunderstood what the Bible actually says about false prophets. Some critical people mistake the New Testament gift for something closer to the Old Testament version by implying that if it comes from God, then it is infallible so nothing can stop it. The flipside of this is that they imply that you are a false prophet if one thing that you say does not come to pass.

If you study false prophecy, that is not the correct way of testing. The main test for a false prophet was to determine *which* god they told their audience to follow. If it was not the one true God, then you could dismiss them. Contrary to what some people think, inaccuracy is not a sign of a false prophet. Inaccuracy regarding prophecy is mentioned in the Bible because we are human. Incomplete prophecy does not equal inaccurate prophecy!

"For we know in part and we prophesy in part."
1 Corinthians 13:9

In the Old Testament, false prophecy had to do with people who were leading Israel to worship other gods. (Deuteronomy 13:1–5) False prophets tried to lead God's people to worship strange gods and there is a huge difference between that and prophesying *in part.*

The New Testament encourages us to be open and embracing of the prophetic as we see in these Bible verses:

"Follow the way of love and eagerly desire gifts of the Spirit, especially prophecy." 1 Corinthians 14:1

"Do not quench the Spirit. Do not treat prophecies with contempt but test them all; hold on to what is good." 1 Thessalonians 5:19–21

Keep in mind that some prophetic words can seem to be inaccurate, but we do not understand the timing of them, so they do not come to pass or we misinterpret what God is saying. This does not make the person who gave you the prophetic word a false prophet. The way that God speaks is often mysterious and sometimes complicated. We need to be open to change and understand the fact that we can misinterpret or misunderstand what God is saying to us. But we can choose to use these times as learning experiences.

Yes, it is possible that a person can be a false prophet who is trying to lead people to listen to *them* instead of God. Also there are people who are listening to God, but they might not always be accurate in their prophetic words. So be sure that you are testing it in a positive light, and yes, you do want to discern the source. You discern the source by writing it down and listening to what God says about it. I cannot say it enough: it is good to write it down! When discerning God's voice, it will soon become a habit if you begin to do this. It takes both time and effort, and it is worth it.

HOW GOD SPEAKS AND HOW TO RESPOND

"For God may speak in one way, or in another, yet man does not perceive it. In a dream, in a vision of the night, when deep sleep falls upon men, while slumbering on their beds, then He opens the ears of men, and seals their instruction. In order to turn man from his deed, and conceal pride from man." Job 33:14–17 NKJV

How good is that? God can and will speak to you even if you do not perceive or understand it. He can conceal away revelation from your natural mind to keep you from getting prideful. God is often sealing our instructions even though we are not aware of it.

Later we can live out these hidden things that God has given us in our spirits and our lives are changed by it.

The point is that you do not always have to understand or remember things in your mind for God to speak and change your life.

Dreams, Words, Friends And Angels

God can speak through a dream, a friend, a movie—even a TV commercial! And He can speak through a prophetic word because there is nothing He cannot use. All of these ways apply. Everything applies!

It is the same principle whether it is a dream you have had, or it is something that you hear a friend share with you through the Holy Spirit. Many find that the Holy Spirit speaks directly to their spirit during times of prayer. The takeaway is that God may use anything He chooses in order to seal your instructions, keep you from pride and keep you moving in the right direction.

God can also speak through one of His angels. In the book of Acts, there is a lot of angelic activity. In Acts 8:26, Phillip has an encounter with an angel and the angel tells him where to travel next. In verse twenty-nine, the Spirit tells Phillip how to respond. He meets a man who is pondering the meaning of a verse in the Book of Isaiah. Phillip explains the passage and tells him about Jesus. The man believes and is baptized. God used a combination of a messenger angel and the Holy Spirit to speak to Phillip because He wanted to bring a single person into the Kingdom.

Parables And God's Hidden Language

God can speak through parables and other Bible verses, popular movies, music and of course, the prophetic gifts. Let's talk about hearing God through the prophetic or revelatory gifts. Because God's methods are so varied and not limited in any way, what we need to understand is the *way* God speaks, that is, God's hidden language.

How do we learn this language? I have found that it really helps to read the parables. When you do, you will begin to understand that not only is God speaking all the time, He often uses everyday situations as a starting point for people to receive a deeper spiritual message.

"It is the glory of God to conceal a matter, But the glory of kings is to search out a matter." Proverbs 25:2 NKJV

When we talk about activating your prophetic word, it is based on this Proverb. It is about learning to *search out the matter.*

Think about the last time you had to really search for something. It probably took some time and effort. It may have even taken some outside help. It is the same with searching out the meaning and direction of a prophetic word.

Compared to prophetic words, dreams can be a little harder to understand, even if you have studied and taken courses. I have gotten a lot of training in dream interpretation over the years and I have interpreted a lot of dreams—more than I can count!

Studying the parables will help you see how God uses metaphors as you consider the symbols and settings you see in dreams.

When it comes to the prophetic gifts, it really does take time to learn to discern, because it is about getting to know God and how He talks to you personally. It is helpful to slow down and record things that you hear and experience, and then pray and ask God to show you what is for now and what is for later.

I am really excited that you have chosen to work through this book and my other training materials because it will help you get started. Also, if you have been using your prophetic gifts for a long time, this can help you get to a new level.

God Speaks To You, What Now?

Let's say you had a dream that seems significant, or perhaps someone contacted you out of the blue to share a Bible verse that they thought might encourage you. Maybe you felt strangely moved by a movie you watched, and you cannot seem to shake the feeling that maybe God is trying to tell you something. What do you do now?

Write It Down

The best way to start is to write it down. Write down your prophetic word or dream. This is the first thing you will want to do. I believe that we should record prophetic words whenever possible. If you receive a prophetic word from someone and you can record it on your cell phone or recorder, then do it. Do whatever it takes to save it. If possible, download it to your computer so that you can listen to it again. I would suggest you transcribe your prophesy. If it is long, you can break it into manageable paragraphs.

Look up Bible references, and consider doing a word study or other related Bible research into the themes God shows you. Look up key words in the dictionary and encyclopedia; use anything that helps

27

you grasp the depth of meaning. Listen to the word several times and ask the Holy Spirit to speak to you. Take some notes. Ask God questions. Search the matter out!

How To Respond To A Prophetic Word

It helps to realize that simply because God has spoken, it is not somehow *automatic,* or guaranteed to happen. When God speaks, it is very important that you understand the timing. In other words, is this for now, or for five years from now?

Also keep in mind that you may need to take into account that the word is coming through your filter or someone else's. Some prophetic words represent God's intention for you, but you will need to contend or battle through to get it.

In 1 Corinthians 13:9 the apostle Paul said, *"For we know in part and we prophesy in part."* So do not expect the prophetic word to contain everything God wants to say to you. It is also very important that you take the time to *test* the word. (1 Thessalonians 5:19–21) It is good to test the prophetic word to see if there is anything in it that is cloudy, unclear or even jarring. A lot of people do not understand what testing a word means.

They may ask, "Where is that in the Bible?" because they believe that every prophetic word must literally be found word for word in the Bible or they throw the whole thing out.

This is not a good method for testing prophetic words because it is just too narrow. This way does not take into account all the other ways God uses to speak to us! What we are talking about is discovering a biblical principle for growing in our understanding and not limiting how we will receive that word from God.

To test a word, it helps to avoid judging in a negative way. Start by praying and asking God to show you first of all if there are things in the prophetic word that are not in agreement with biblical principles. You may need to discount anything that goes against the ways and character of God, anything about Him being unloving or that will bring harm. God would never give someone a word that would purposely take him or her off track.

Keep in mind, though, that some prophetic words might challenge or stretch us in our understanding. What is most important to remember is that God really does speak and our part is to train ourselves to notice, pray and then grab hold of it. Prophetic words often require action on our part to activate them.

Journaling Is A Key To Hearing God

People ask me how do you journal every day? Let me just give you some tips on journaling. These are things I do all the time. When people think of journaling they get the image of regurgitating your emotions into a *dear diary* format. I do not just write long pages about what I am feeling, thinking, doing, dreaming and hearing. I use bullet points. I quickly describe whatever I want to reflect on so that I can recall it in more detail later. You can do whatever works for you. You can draw, use different colors, even different types of pens and paper. The more it reflects you and your personality, the more you will be drawn back to it.

Journaling software is my go-to method and has been for quite a few years. The reason I use computers is because for a long time I used to write everything down by hand. I now have a pile of written journals that is literally three-feet high. I used paper journals all the way up to 2006. At that point, good computer journals started to become available and I switched to a computer.

I really like it because you can actually do a search for the word *angel,* or search for something else you wanted to follow up on and find all the entries that reference that word or phrase. You can also tag and cross reference things. It is excellent for writers and teachers who like to return to their notes and develop material from their insights and experience. I just like it better. Here is the key thing to successful journaling—do what is most natural to you, whatever that may be. Remember, you do not have to do what I do, but do what fits for you, and most importantly, what is going to work.

Tips On Revelation Mining

I start my journal every day by reading my own *Daily Prophetic Word* that comes by email. This is the one I release to everyone. You might wonder how those would be fresh to me, since I am the one who wrote them. The reason is because I hear and record them maybe a month or two ahead of time so I do not really remember them when they finally come out. When it shows up in my email, I copy and paste it into my journal. Just doing that gets me into my journal and then I start praying and asking God to speak to me.

Whether someone gives you a prophetic word or you get a prophetic word directly, you will want to start with a bullet-point list. For instance, today I am bullet-pointing some things about what God is speaking to me. The next thing I do is to make sure I review a few days of entries and fill in those bullet points with more details. I do this at least once a week. I recommend that you do that as well.

Look at the previous days and weeks in your journal to see what has become clearer, even in this short amount of time. I go back through my notes from that previous week and start to fill things in because stuff happened that I may not have realized. This is where you start to see where God said something and how it is unfolding. You will be surprised at how many prayers have been answered and that indeed God is speaking to you. It is so exciting!

Now just type or write down what you hear or sense God is saying. You can put in prayer requests and go back and update it later. It is a lot like mining. I like to call it *revelation mining*. We are going to go in and mine the riches you can find there. Did you know that wisdom and understanding are the riches of the Kingdom? It is true. It is a lot like that. Have you ever seen those reality TV shows about the Gold Rush? The idea is that they are sitting right on top of millions of dollars, but first they have to locate and mine it. It is a process, but with practice, you will find it begins to come more easily.

It is the same with revelation. We are sitting on revelation right now. God is ready and He is willing. God is speaking right now but most people are not mining for it. In Job 33:14–17, God speaks in one way or another, but men and women do not always understand it, because they have not put their attention to it.

The good news is the Holy Spirit is in you, and you have access to everything you need to succeed as far as the ability to hear God. (John 10:27) I just want to say this: you have it all and God has given it to you.

His Word says that all things are possible for those who believe. (Mark 9:23) You can do all things through

Christ who gives you strength. (Philippians 4:13) You have the Holy Spirit in you. God created the Heavens and the Earth, and He created you in His image, therefore you are creative and you have all the resources that you could possibly need. You just have to tap into them.

LEARNING TO DISCERN

"But seek first his kingdom and his righteousness, and all these things will be given to you as well." Matthew 6:33

The foundation I am talking about is found in Matthew 6:33. When we are looking for a prophetic word from God, sometimes we look outside ourselves because we want things to come into our life and there is nothing wrong with that. There are things that we all need in our life.

Yet some people judge the prophetic gifts as unnecessary and say, "All you need is Jesus" or "All you need is the Word of God." Did you know that there are examples of people getting prophetic words throughout the Bible?

In 1 Samuel 16:12, the prophet Samuel sees young David and God declares him to be the next king by saying, *"this is the one!"*

In Acts 21:4, there are disciples who warn Paul *"through the Spirit"* not to go to Jerusalem. God speaks and when this happens, the prophetic word brings hope and encouragement. It can bring confirmation and direction. We need a balance of hearing God through the Bible and also through the ways the Holy Spirit chooses to speak to us.

Healing Of Prophetic Hopelessness

I have seen a condition that has set into the Church and into Christians' lives that the Bible calls *hope deferred.*

"Hope deferred makes the heart sick, but a longing fulfilled is a tree of life." Proverbs 13:12

I base my prophetic words on hope. The very reason my prophetic words are positive and encouraging is to help bring healing to the heartbroken condition people suffer when their hope has been deferred.

When someone gets a prophetic word that does not seem to come about in their life they can suffer from *prophetic hopelessness* and often give up on hearing the voice of God. That is what people need right now; people need their longings fulfilled and their hope in God restored.

Avoiding Prophetic Shipwrecks

To be clear, not all prophetic words are meant for right now. A common mistake a lot of people make is when they receive a prophetic word, instead of waiting and testing it, they act on it too soon in the form of some major decision.

For instance, I have seen people shipwreck themselves because they believed God told them that they are going to have a ministry. So they go out and buy a $10,000 website and make a bunch of decisions before they have anything in place. Or God spoke to them and said that they are going to have a business so they go out and buy something right away by faith, trying to activate it.

It is true that you usually need to work your way into it, and you use Godly wisdom. You have to use both wisdom and understanding.

That is one of my prayers for you. My prayer is that you would understand the timing of what you have heard from God. At the same time, it is important to activate or respond to it in some way. It is biblical to do something practical along the way. I encourage people to do something to activate their prophetic words, but do not go bankrupt doing it.

Quite often, when we get a prophetic word, we need to wait on God for timing on what to do with it. But as you will find in this book, there are things you can do now to activate and prepare for the things that God is speaking. You can wait on God, but you do not have to be passive. You can be proactive and do things to prepare for the future.

That is not to say that there are not things that you can do right away. There are! Just start to activate it. What does that look like? I will give you an example from my life. Because I have learned to hear God on a regular basis, I am rarely surprised by the words given to me anymore. Yet a few months ago, I got a world-rocking prophetic word from someone. Most words people give me are confirming and comforting words, but I got this one and it really shocked me. It was an astonishing word and it was very accurate. I wanted to activate it and so I applied some of the same principles and exercises that I have shared in this book

One of the first things I did was to write it down. Fortunately I also had it recorded, so I had it transcribed. After that I got together with some intercessors and shared it with some other people I trust. We began to break it down to understand it better. We prayed about it and even found some *declarations* from the Bible. These are verses that go along with a few of the main bullet points of the prophetic word. We began to pull those in to pray and declare things that are not as though they are (Romans 4:17), declaring the prophetic word and believing.

"You will also decree a thing, and it will be established for you; And light will shine on your ways." Job 22:28 NASB

Making declarations is very powerful as it brings your prophetic word into alignment with God's written Word. Once I understood what God was speaking to me, I took this a step further and did something practical to activate it. In my case, God was calling me to find people whom I could delegate areas of my ministry to in order to free me up to write, speak and coach. So I created job descriptions then began praying and seeking. There are different ways you can do that. This is how I usually do it. This was a several month process.

An update on this, my ministry is now thriving and I have an amazing team that is helping me. I have a newfound freedom and creativeness to write books like this one. It was not easy hiring the new people. We had to take steps of faith for the finances and there were several people that did not work out along the way. So it was a stretching and painful process such as when you birth something new. But it all came about after hearing God and activating what I was hearing.

Hearing God Requires Belief

One of the biggest things to do for activation is to believe. Hearing God requires belief. What do I mean by that? Well, unbelief was one of the main things that shut Jesus down from doing miracles. (Mark 6:5) We need to be sure that we do not have doubt and unbelief hiding somewhere in our lives. Yes, you might believe that God speaks today, but you might not believe that He wants to speak to you as clearly as what I am describing.

It requires a trust and dependence on God. It means belief in God's character and knowing that He really is who He says He is. God is a father to the fatherless. He defends the widow and the orphan. His

Word is meant to light your way so that you can see where you are going. (Psalm 119:105) God's heart for you is that you prosper, and His intention is never to harm you. (Jeremiah 29:11) Believing that God speaks, that He is speaking to you, that you matter and taking time to listen to Him is so important!

Spend Time Listening

When we spend time listening to God, it shows that we value what God says. We need to consider it precious. We do not treat it lightly. When we talk about activating, it is about responding in some way. It is so important to take the time to listen to God. God told me one day a while back that I was doing too much talking during my prayer times. He wants to give us solutions to our prayers, but at times we need to be quiet and listen. A lot of times we get into prayer mode and we are commanding things and we are claiming the Word, but there are times when we need to take time, slow down, take a deep breath and learn to simply listen to what He is saying.

One of the ways to do that is to purposely make time each day to not only spend time reading the Bible (that is good), and not just spend time in prayer (though that is also good), but to also listen. It is important to spend time simply listening to God. Take a walk or a drive, or whatever you need to do in order to get in a place where you are not going to be interrupted or distracted. Most people hear God in the shower more than anywhere else because it is one of the few places that they will not be interrupted and they are relatively relaxed.

Practice Hearing

I know I mentioned this already and I might say it again, but the importance of hearing God clearly is to practice. Make listening to God a regular thing that you do. When I first started practicing hearing God, many people at my church and some of my close friends thought it was acceptable to do during ministry times only. But when I started going with others out to public places like the mall to practice, they thought it was wrong. One leader told me it was too much like fortune telling. I had to beg to differ. Fortune telling is not done through the Holy Spirit. God wants us to hear His voice. We are allowed to practice all the other gifts mentioned in the Bible, but for some reason prophecy has been placed on a higher pedestal.

When it comes to hearing God and maturing, Hebrews 5:14 really says it best. It is by the *"constant use"* (in other words, practice) of hearing God, that you can make a habit of using your spiritual gifts, and you can train yourself *"to distinguish good from evil."*

Some people ask me, "How can you know that what you are hearing is from God, from yourself, or from the enemy?" Is it possible to "learn to discern?" The answer is yes, you can.

The only way I have figured out how to do that is to write it down and to journal. I have found that the most effective way to test anything I think I am hearing from God is to immediately put it in my journal and record the date. This applies (in no particular order) to dreams, pictures, visions, His still small voice, angelic visitations, Bible verses that seem magnified to me and prophetic words that others give to me.

I have found the best way that you can learn to discern is to go back to one of the times that you *know* that you heard God or that He answered one of your prayers, and study it. How did it come to you? What did it feel like?

43

You have got to actually grab hold of what the authentic feels like so that you will recognize the counterfeit. Developing a basic prophetic word journal will help you track what God is saying to you.

Focus On God and Not Demons

I mentioned grabbing hold of the authentic so you will recognize the counterfeit. Unfortunately, some people today are actually too focused on the counterfeit. They are more focused on demons than they are on angels or the Holy Spirit.

How do I know this? Because I have had encounters with angels and when I start talking about it at a church or in a meeting people get uncomfortable.

The odd thing is if I said, "I think there is a demon in the room," then probably 95% of these people would say, "Yes, I agree." This is a sad day when discerning demons is actually of higher value than discerning what the Holy Spirit or angels are doing in the room and that is where we need to flip this around.

This is exactly what I do in my training. I have been committed now, for years, to help people understand the goodness and loving ways of God and to move the focus away from the enemy. Do you know that being overly focused on the negative is not going to get us where we want to be?

Again, what I have discovered is if you want to learn to discern, then practice going back to one of the times that you have heard God clearly. When you study in that way, you will harness that memory, and the recognition of God's voice. Then when something new comes, you will start to recognize how it feels. Before you know it you will recognize more and more how God speaks. You will build a history with Him and your journal will become a learning log. He will relate to you personally, speaking in ways that make sense to you because He knows you and wants you to understand!

Did you know that the toughest part is not discerning good from evil? That is actually pretty easy. Discerning the difference between yourself and God is a little tougher than recognizing the enemy. The things that come from the enemy tend to have a certain essence to it. It will have a prideful aspect to it. There are ways to discern this. You can learn all of this though it takes practice. All I can tell you is practice, and that is why I journal 365 days a year. It does not mean that you have to you have to journal, but the reality is, if you are not writing things down, then you are not practicing, which means you are probably not able to learn to discern at the level that you need to.

It Takes Practice And Time

You know what shocks me? It is how much time and effort some people spend on their hobbies, jobs and entertainment. When it comes to learning to discern, more people are better at trivia than they are at their ability to hear God. There are more people who are better at their golf game.

Why? Because they have actually practiced and hired coaches and they have done all kinds of things to improve. But how many people actually do that for their spiritual gifts?

That is why I am a prophetic life coach, offer online activation schools and why I wrote this book. I want to coach you in your ability to discern. Hearing God is easy enough that a child can do it. It will take practice if you want to get better at it, which means it will take time and effort. It takes as much time and practice to master your prophetic gifts as it does to develop other skills. Think of the time you are willing to put into your sport, your kids' sports or learning a musical instrument that you want to play well.

I am a musician and I know what it means to practice. I played guitar for a number of years and those chords did not come automatically until I practiced every day, or at least a few times a week. After a while it started to come automatically. If you want to learn to discern, start to practice and very soon it will become automatic. You will learn to discern and then you will be able to help other people along the way.

Did you know that teaching and helping others strengthens our own expertise? It is so exciting when you realize how God speaks and how He works everything together for our good. The kind of practice that I am talking about does not need to take a long time. You can do small amounts at a time, but the key is consistency.

RESPONDING TO GOD SPEAKING

Daily Prophetic Words

Here is an example from my life that has helped me understand how God speaks. A few years ago I felt impressed to ask God for short, encouraging words that I can post on various social media sites each day. The purpose was to show people how God can speak to you each day so they can learn to respond and activate it in their lives.

I began writing what God shows me and I call them *Daily Prophetic Words.* For the most part these prophetic words are what I would call *confirming* words. Most of the time people have already sensed God speaking the same message to them before they read the encouraging word. So there is a sort of *echo* to the prophetic word where God is repeating Himself to reassure people that they have heard Him accurately.

I have them posted on my website, as well as on Twitter, Facebook, and Instagram if you would like to see examples. It is not like these are weighty prophetic words. Most are words of knowledge (you will find these explained in 1 Corinthians 12). These prophetic words are usually about the present or the past and some are a bit about the future.

The *Daily Prophetic Words* are very short because I release them on Twitter and social media sites that have a limit on the number of characters you can use. I generally get them a month or more in advance, one for each day of the month. They are not for every person on every day. But more times than not, God uses the *Daily Prophetic Words* to speak to people and give them encouragement. I am often surprised when I read them each day.

Prophetic Blogs And Articles

I also release weekly and monthly prophetic words through my Internet blog on my website. These are actually much more prophetic in nature; they are, about the future as well as encouraging. God has gifted me to understand the times and seasons. So my weekly and monthly prophetic articles often contain specific dates and periods of time. I basically report what God speaks to me about the specific season that we are in as a Church or people at large. Again, it might not apply to every person, but I get a lot of feedback that it is exactly what masses of people are experiencing.

I invite you to read some of these on my blog. Read some of my prophetic articles too, because it will help you understand the process I go through in how I hear God.

I try to explain as much as I can about how these words come to me. I try to let people know that it is not always so mystical to hear God. It actually becomes naturally supernatural when you grab hold of the ability to hear God on a daily basis. I try to demystify it and to really activate people into recognizing the fact that God is speaking all the time and most of us are missing it.

It is really important for us to understand who God is. We can hold up the prophetic words we receive and compare them to what we know of God's character and see if they match up. This is comforting to know—God will never leave us or forsake us. He does not bring us out so far and then leave us hanging. So, as we set out to know this, remember that it takes time, and the great thing is that it is time well spent.

"But Jesus often withdrew to lonely places and prayed."
Luke 5:16

We can set aside time to pray through things and begin to get a hold of them. Even in lonely places and seasons we are never truly alone. God is always leading us, helping us along the way.

"But I'll take the hand of those who don't know the way, who can't see where they're going. I'll be a personal guide to them, directing them through unknown country. I'll be right there to show them what roads to take, make sure they don't fall into the ditch. These are the things I'll be doing for them—sticking with them, not leaving them for a minute." Isaiah 42:16 MSG

Remember To Respond

The next thing is to remember to respond to a prophetic word. We must respond in order to remove our hindrances to hearing God. Our own theology can even stop us, especially if we believe God only speaks in a certain way. If God is calling you to something new, sometimes what you believe can get in the way. God wants to help us where we do not yet trust Him to do things we have never seen before. He delights to show us His ways. Presumption or assuming that you know what He is saying can be a hindrance too. If you are trying to find something new, busyness is another thing that will keep you from hearing God.

When God calls us to do something new, we often have to forget the former ways that we did things. This is usually very difficult for us to do. But, it is our old way of thinking and doing things that can hinder our progress; and this is the very reason we need to hear God for something new. God changes the seasons in our lives and what worked in a previous season might not work now.

"Forget the former things; do not dwell on the past. See, I am doing a new thing! Now it springs up; do you not perceive it? I am making a way in the wilderness and streams in the wasteland." Isaiah 43:18–19

This can be easier said than done, but if you commit to developing yourself personally and are ready to let go of beliefs and choices that may be hindering you, you will do well. That is why I wrote the book *Personal Development God's Way*. Because God showed me that we all need a way to be able to develop ourselves, just as we do with our sports and hobbies.

As I said earlier, most people put more effort into those things than they do in developing their ability to hear God.

God is doing something new right now. I believe that if you put yourself out there to learn to discern, and if you ask God to speak to you, He will. Then as you begin to record what you hear, God will answer you and you will be more ready than ever to hear and respond.

Judging Versus Positively Testing

Let's talk more about how to judge a prophetic word. In 1 Thessalonians 5:19–22, Paul says, *"Do not quench the Spirit. Do not treat prophecies with contempt but test them all; hold on to what is good, reject every kind of evil."*

I think there is a misunderstanding about how to judge a prophetic word. It tends to be thought of as a negative thing as opposed to objectively looking at it and weighing it out.

"But solid food is for the mature, who by constant use have trained themselves to distinguish good from evil." Hebrews 5:14

What this book is designed to do is to give you the tools to train yourself to distinguish good from evil, and to be able to recognize a prophetic word. Not only that, but it will help you know how to act on it. When you learn how to activate a word, you will know what to do and when to do it.

Discernment Comes With Maturity

I have been hearing God all my life, but it was not until the last ten years or so that I started to learn to discern. There are a couple of schools of thought out there about how God speaks. One school of thought (it is an older school of thought) believes that God only needs to speak to you. That is it. You do not have to discern or interpret. God will just speak to you in a dictation method. All you have to do is listen and receive. There is no interpretation or explanation needed.

Let me clarify, I am talking about God speaking to you directly through the Holy Spirit. It might come to you in many forms, but it is how you respond to what you are hearing that really makes a difference. I believe in activating what we hear from God. The older school of thought makes us more like robots in which we hear and then obey. This was needed years ago during a time in which people needed more specific direction. But now God is calling us to be living sons and daughters who are allowed to interact with their loving Father in Heaven. The season has changed and so has the way in which we can respond.

The Open Door Strategy Can Be Dangerous

"I will instruct you and teach you in the way you should go; I will counsel you with my loving eye on you." Psalms 32:8

A mistake people often make in trying to hear God for guidance in decisions is by using the *open door* strategy. Many people pray that God will close all other doors of opportunity except the one they should go through. This may work sometimes, but unfortunately, it does not always happen that way with God. He wants us to become mature in our decision-making, so He will often give us choices to train us.

It is like the way an earthly father helps his children. You cannot make decisions for them all their life, or they never grow up. A better way to pray is that God will give you the wisdom to know which opportunity or door to take. Hear me, I am not saying that the open door strategy does not work. I am saying that the seasons are changing and God wants us to learn to discern and know how to respond.

Most often people will default to using the "fleece technique" from Judges 6. Gideon asked God for a sign that He was with him. Gideon laid a fleece of wool on the ground and asked that the fleece would be wet and the ground dry. Sure enough, the next morning he found it wet and the ground dry. So he knew God had answered him.

It is possible for God to answer these types of prayers. "God, if it is your desire for me to do this, then make this happen …" Again, God wants us to become mature in our decision making. Eventually God may not answer one of these prayers, and you will need to rely on other means of determining His will. Since the Holy Spirit is now in us, unlike in Gideon's day, we now can know God's will by the amount of peace we have. God's will always comes with His peace. Peace is the best fleece!

A friend of mine was trying to decide what area to live in and which house to buy. He relied heavily on the "open door" strategy and asked God to close all other doors except the house he should buy. He bought a house and lost a lot of money in the process. It is important to understand how God speaks to us and how to respond, especially for major decisions.

Using Prophecy For Major Decisions

Remember this: when you go to test a prophetic word and there is a major life decision to be made in response to it, it is best not to think in terms of a list of pros and cons or methods like that. That is more like reasoning than discernment. There is nothing wrong with reasoning, but if God decides to call you to something new, and He gives you a prophetic word about it (even if it is a matter of confirmation), you will still want to get more than one piece of revelation for something major in your life.

What you are looking for would be more like a *witness*. What is a witness? In basic terms, a witness is someone who can confirm that something happened. Now, if you are looking at a major life change, such as a job change, a move, a large purchase, then invest some time in asking and hearing God for a confirming word.

It is not wise to make major life decisions on the basis of a single word or dream. God will confirm things, and you will get more. And that is what is required for the greater things.

Watch for God to provide a witness, another *yes* to outweigh the uncertainty. He is faithful and wants you to trust that He is speaking to you.

Do Not Worry

As you are learning to test these things out just remember that it will not always feel easy. When God calls you to change, it might not be comfortable.

This is where some people might use "pros and cons" when deciding whether to move ahead with what they are sensing God is telling them.

"And let the peace (soul harmony which comes) from Christ rule (act as umpire continually) in your hearts [deciding and settling with finality all questions that arise in your minds, in that peaceful state] to which as [members of Christ's] one body you were also called [to live]. And be thankful (appreciative), [giving praise to God always]." Colossians 3:15 AMPC

When I look for a confirmation from the Lord, I look for peace, because the enemy cannot duplicate peace. Do not get me wrong, sometimes things are not as clear. It can feel so subjective. You do not really have to worry about messing up though, because we all make mistakes as we learn. That is what learning is! The wonderful thing is that even as you make mistakes, God has grace for you and will use them to train you.

And realize this, God is always doing something on a greater level. He is doing something bigger, and He is trying to instill Kingdom principles into you. He is trying to draw you to Himself. He is trying to get you to understand His ways of intimacy, and He is trying to show you that He is a loving father and not a judge ready to nuke you.

IMPORTANCE OF TRAINING

I have trained thousands of people to hear the voice of God over the years. I have noticed a recent change in the way God is speaking to people. It used to be that God would dictate prophetic words and instructions to us and we would repeat them to someone word-for-word. Let me be clear that this approach may be easier to do for certain people who tend to be more prophetically gifted. By that I mean, the prophetic gifts would be their stronger gifts, or the ones that are easier for them to operate in.

Some of the newer ways that God is speaking to people is in the form of people seeing, sensing or feeling what God is saying as opposed to hearing it word-for-word. The sensor-feeler types of prophetic people can hear what God is saying, but it often needs to be explained or interpreted instead of dictated. I happen to operate in all of these styles. There are times that God speaks to me in a dictation mode and then I see a picture over a person or get a strong sense or feeling in my spirit that has to be interpreted or explained.

There are all types of gifts. In 1 Corinthians 12, Paul goes into many of the various types of spiritual gifts that God gives to people. If you happen to be prophetically gifted, it is easy to operate in the "hearing dictation" style of giving prophetic words. I can understand that thinking, because it is how I was trained to do it. I hear God, I receive it, and then I say to the person what I am hearing.

But what many do not realize, is that there are other people whose gift mix is different and they are in a process of strengthening and developing their ability to hear the voice of God. Paul said to *"… eagerly desire gifts of the Spirit, especially prophecy."* (1 Corinthians 14:1)

We all have access to all the spiritual gifts through the Holy Spirit. You might operate in one gift more than another, but if you look at the life of Jesus and His disciples, you will see that they all operated in all the gifts.

Suppose, for the sake of argument, that I said ten percent of Christians are prophetically gifted. That would mean ninety percent of people would not process prophetic words the way this school of thought teaches. They simply would not understand it. It would be like saying to a prophetically gifted person, "Hey, just get up and teach, sing a song or administrate." We need to take into account a person's gift mix and how God speaks to them uniquely.

Indeed we need training in the areas that are not our strongest gift. It is good to study and develop all your spiritual gifts, no matter how strong they are in your life. No gift is better than the others. We develop them all through the Holy Spirit as we mature, and according to where God has us.

This is the reason that over the years most prophetic training has been done by those with the prophetic gifting as their primary gift. They have always heard God, and did not necessarily have to be trained.

As a result, there have been a lot of assumptions about how God speaks that do not make sense to everyone who wants to learn more. Even though I have lived my life being able to hear God fairly easily, what I am trying to do is help you develop the *eyes that see* and *ears that hear* how God may be speaking to you, no matter what your primary gifting may be. And God speaks in so many different ways! He will speak to a person with a teaching gift more through the Bible and with instructions. To a worshiper, He will speak more through things like songs and the arts.

Most of the prophetic training in the past taught, God speaks and then you wait on Him to open the door or bring it about in your life. You cannot do anything but wait.

This type of thinking has actually derailed many people in the church today because they have been waiting for God to show up when in many cases it takes action on their part. If you read these accounts in the Bible where people had to take action, they actually had to do things with what they received from God to bring it about.

There are some cases where it is true that God is the only one who can open the door for certain things. We cannot just put a blanket statement out there because hearing God is very subjective, and it is unique to each person's situation. That is why I want to encourage you to study how God speaks to *you* and take notes or journal. When you take notes and study how God speaks to you, you will learn to discern and be able to open up things like never before.

A Need For Training

It was not until I decided to study my gifts on a deeper level years ago that I started using some of the things that I am about to share with you. The prophetic gift tends to be one of the gifts that, in my view, we do not study as much.

If you are called to teaching, there is a lot of teacher training; if you are called to administrate there is a lot of training on how to organize and how to be a project manager; and if you are called to hospitality, wow, there is a whole television empire called the Food Network out there for hospitality training purposes.

But if you are prophetic, there has only been the "school of the prophets" type of training in which prophets train other people who feel called to be prophets. But God is speaking more now through all the spiritual gifts. We need new training that will help everyone hear the voice of God through their unique spiritual gifts. I have been developing new training courses and schools to help people with this. Even the idea of activating your prophetic word might sound strange to those who came up during the older ways of prophetic training.

I remember when I first started doing this that people in my church thought I was strange. I have always been multi-gifted and I joke that I am like a "Swiss Army Knife" with my spiritual gifts. I started out as an intercessor back in the 1980s. I was using my prophetic gifts to do prophetic intercession. Today there is a lot of training for prophetic intercessors, but back then there was not. I would pray, get a prophetic word and then because I was a practical administration type as well, I would tell others and we would do something practical to activate what God was saying. Over the years, people told me that I should not be doing that. They told me that I should just wait for God to speak to me, wait for Him to open the door and obey what He tells me to do.

But this is a new time and season. We are moving into a time when God is speaking to us all the time. He speaks 24/7! I go into a lot of churches to teach and train. In fact, I was at 150 meetings per year over an eleven-year period. I took notes over that time and I noticed that during worship a lot of people would stop and then wait. And wait. There would be a moment of silence and everything would just pause. There nothing wrong with it, but someone who is new might wonder, "What is going on?" "Well, we are waiting on God." "Why? Is He late?"

Why are we always waiting on God? What I realized is that we are not really waiting on God; He is always there. We are waiting on ourselves to catch on to what He is doing. For most people it takes time and practice. We have to get into His timing. And I have learned to step into that doorway. That spiritual door is right in front of you all the time and with practice you can enter into it without having to have an hour or more of worship.

I often go into churches that do a very long worship set before I am going to speak. I love worship, but since I have discovered that we can live under an open Heaven of God's presence, I no longer need long times of preparing myself. So I usually start taking notes of what I am hearing from the Holy Spirit before I go into the meeting.

At one church someone turned to me and asked, "Why are you not entering into the worship?" I replied, "I am already in. As a matter of fact, I came into the room already in the presence of God." Some people are not aware that there is even a doorway that we can enter and many are not aware that we can enter into it quickly. We need to be trained on how to do this because there are times in which we need to hear God for our situations, but we might not be in a long worship service to get there.

Know Which Door To Take

In Revelation 3:20 Jesus says, *"Here I am! I stand at the door and knock. If anyone hears my voice and opens the door, I will come in and eat with that person, and they with me."* In that situation, Jesus says, *"I stand at the door and knock. If anyone ... opens the door ..."* Do you hear that?

This is not like Matthew 7:7 which is a case where there is another door. *"Ask and it will be given to you; seek and you will find; knock and the door will be opened to you."*

Now look at that. Matthew 7:7 says the door will be opened to you, whereas in Revelation 3:20, you have to open the door. In order for God to open the door, according to Matthew 7:7–you have to be proactive. It says, ask, seek and knock. Notice that it is an acronym: ASK, as in ask, seek and knock. That is very proactive!

It does not say to "Sit on the couch, and wait for God to open the door." It does not say you should "Take time off from your job and wait for God to speak to you." It does not say any of those things that many people are doing in order to hear God's voice.

When we ask, we use our voice. When we seek, we use our minds. And when we knock, we use our hands. Not only is it not a passive process, it engages all of who we are: body, soul and spirit. I am not being judgmental. What I am saying is, "We need a breakthrough today." And yes, there are some things where you will need to wait on God to open the door. There are always greater things that you will need to wait on.

While you are waiting you need to go back to the very last thing or other things that God told you to do, and do them. Avoid waiting passively. This will train you and build you up. When we become passive and go into isolation waiting on God to open a door for us the enemy can use this to bring depression and the loss of our vision.

I minister to people all the time who have not been trained in how to understand and properly interpret what God is saying. There are so many people over-responding or misinterpreting what God is saying. In a sense, instead of activating what God is saying, they are deactivating it by getting out of His timing or by doing things that He did not tell them to do. This is why we need training, activation and confirmation.

HOW TO TEST A PROPHETIC WORD

There are a lot of things that you can do right now that will prepare you for the future. And you can start getting ready right now based on how God speaks to you. One of the things that I hear a lot when people first receive a prophetic word is, "I have to judge that word. I have to test it against the Word of God," which is true. We do need to test our prophetic words against the Word of God.

I have been talking about many ways already on how to test and activate a prophetic word. Here is the thing: as God begins to speak to you, you do need to be able to judge those words. You need to be able to discern them, but the word *judging* sounds judgmental. No matter what we call it, we do need to be careful that when we go to test, weigh, discern or judge a word, that we are not doing it in a negative way.

Testing a word involves asking or objectively looking at a few things. Does it line up with the Bible? Has God spoken something similar to you before?

71

How does it feel in your spirit? Does it hit you in a positive or negative way? Sometimes God is calling you to change, and it will feel different.

So be open about an initial reaction you may have, whether positive or negative, because when we are resistant to change we may react negatively at first. What will help is if you focus on discerning from your spirit, not based on how your mind feels about it.

God created us with a body, soul and spirit. Your mind is part of your soul, which can sometimes trick you. How does your spirit feel? Is there peace? Does it reverberate back? Is there something redemptive in it? Remember, sometimes God wants us to change, and it will not always feel good. It is going to stretch you. The only way you will be able to master your ability to discern is with practice. But if you are practicing from a negative mindset then chances are, you might not be hearing God clearly on a consistent basis.

More On Testing

Here is another thing to look for. Do you know the person who gave the prophetic word to you? Is there positive fruit or evidence of the Holy Spirit in their life? Of course God can speak through anybody. He spoke through Balaam's donkey for instance. It is okay to look at the fruit in their life. Now it does not mean that they are more guaranteed to hear clearly either, so we need to be patient and listen for more confirmation from God.

Have you ever met people who display somewhat questionable character traits and yet they are the ones that can hear God really clearly? Why is that? Oftentimes what happens is when you have the gift of prophecy, you will experience a lifetime of rejection. And a lot of people are not being healed. They are being rejected over and over, and they go from church to church giving out prophetic words, but they have not stayed long enough for people to get to know them and help them mature as Christians.

Often what you are seeing is a wounded person who may unintentionally wound or offend others and yet is still able to move in their spiritual gifts. It is a paradox in the Kingdom that someone can appear mature in their spiritual gifts (particularly if they hear God accurately for others), and yet they seem immature, self-centered and childish. They have a hard time trusting people to help them heal because they have been hurt. We see a lot of highly prophetically gifted people end up in this type of wounded cycle.

We need to help people heal and escape that cycle of rejection. Yes, this was me; and years ago I had to come to a place where I got healed of the rejection I experienced as I was growing in my prophetic gift. The more we embrace healing then the more God can use us in this type of gift. If this is you, I encourage you to pursue the process of healing and restoration that God has for you. God wants you in community so that you can release encouraging words. And you may have to work through the rejection which is part of the downside of the prophetic gift.

But do not throw the baby out with the dirty bathwater. There is no need to stop allowing for prophecy in our lives just because some wounded people have used their gifts in a way that might have hurt others. God still speaks today and we need the prophetic gift and prophetically gifted people. I still value the prophetic words that come from some of these highly gifted, yet highly wounded people. I just have to use extra caution to sift through what they are saying to make sure there is not a mixture of their own thoughts or bad experiences.

Ask The Right Questions

Another helpful thing to do is to write down the prophetic word and ask God to help you understand it. First, ask Him to reveal to you if it is a word from Him or not.

Ask for the interpretation: is it for you or for someone else? Is it for prayer, or for sharing with others? Then ask for wisdom and understanding about the timing. Is it for now or is it for later? Quite often when we get a powerful prophetic word, it is exciting. I know I get excited when I hear the Lord clearly.

Prophecy is designed to turn the focus to God and what He is doing, and to the spiritual realm, which is mysterious and full of wonder. It is awesome to be invited in to the mysteries of God. What a privilege!

"Oh, the depth of the riches of the wisdom and knowledge of God!" Romans 11:33a

"Even angels long to look into these things." 1 Peter 1:12b

Keep in mind that God will often speak to you in a powerful way during a season that you really need it.

Most of the time we get very excited and then nothing happens. This is because God gave you the prophetic word to get you through a difficult time and keep you going through the process of refinement.

How To Tell If You Are Properly Testing A Word

Let's go back to objectively testing a word. I have talked a little bit about it already.

Here are some examples to know if you are judging a word critically as opposed to testing it to see if it is from God. Because if you are doing it critically, that is a negative thing and it does not help anyone determine how to respond to God. In fact, it sows doubt, which is the polar opposite of faith.

Here is how to know if you are actually being critical as opposed to being objective. Your attitude is somewhat suspicious. You begin to doubt that the person that is speaking to you is hearing God. You assume they are wrong before they are proven right.

How do you know if you are being oppositional or critical? You may hear yourself saying before thinking, "Where is that in the Bible?" as opposed to asking God to show you or search out the Biblical principles for yourself. (Proverbs 25:2)

We prove what we value by what we invest in. If you value hearing God and how He chooses to speak, then does it not make sense to invest some time into weighing a prophetic word that someone has given to you? You can invest that time in Bible research, prayer and journaling. This shows God that you value His voice in your life.

I give a lot of prophetic words. If the first thing I hear from a person is, "Where is that in the Bible?" I sometimes want to say, "You have a Bible in your hand, and you have Google on your computer or smart phone, please value what is being said and look it up for yourself." What concerns me is when they do not write it down or pray about it. This will cause the prophetic seeds that God wanted to sow into their life to fall on unfruitful soil like in the parable Jesus shared in Matthew 13.

The prophetic side of God is often a mystery and can be very subjective. It is an amazing gift that needs to be developed in us all. With just a little training and instruction we can start seeing fewer prophetic disasters or shipwrecks and more positive experiences. The first step is to understand what God is saying to us. Then we need to interpret it and find ways to respond or activate it. Getting into God's timing is one of the biggest things that will help you.

UNDERSTANDING GOD'S TIMING

An often difficult part of hearing God is understanding if what you are hearing is for now or later. This can only come with practice, along with some trial and error.

Sometimes God will speak to you about something that you are being called to in the future. He may even give you signs that look like it is happening now. But then things change and the opportunity or situation goes away.

This is common with how God speaks with us. He gives you a foretaste of things that are to come like clues on a treasure map. These are designed to point you in the right direction, show you how to prepare and to encourage you along the way. There are a few seasons in your life that you might go through in activating God's prophetic words over your life. Below we will discuss three examples of understanding God's timing.

First, there may be periods of time in your life in which God is teaching you lessons to grow deeper to spiritual maturity. It may seem as though He is holding you back, but in reality He is training you. It is important to recognize these times so that you can work with God and not strive to accomplish something that it is not time for you to do yet.

Second, it helps to be aware of times when God is testing you and wants you to move forward. Most everything that happens to you is designed to get you into a higher level of spiritual maturity. The exception to this is sickness, which is not God's will for you even if you did learn a great lesson from it.

Third, is the aspect of spiritual warfare when you are pursuing the next steps God has for you and you are on target, but demonic forces try to hold you back. In these cases, knowing what is happening with timing is very crucial. This is why I stress the importance of journaling and tracking your timing. The majority of the time you are not able to see these various seasons and understand the bigger picture until later on. Then, it is as if a light is switched on and you have deeper understanding of what is happening and how to respond.

We Need To Contend For More

There will be times when God speaks to us clearly. There will be other times we walk through dry seasons in which we might not hear God or our life is full of the exact opposite of the things He has called us to. This is part of growing and maturing. God wants us to contend and battle for the things He has spoken or promised us. There are stories throughout the Bible of how people have had to do this to obtain the things God has spoken.

Over the years, there have been times that God has spoken to me very clearly about my calling to help people hear His voice, understand their dreams and discover their destiny. In the midst of this, I found myself in seasons in which I needed a breakthrough to get there. Yes, there is a verse in the Bible that God spoke to the apostle Paul, *"My grace is sufficient for you, for my power is made perfect in weakness."* 2 Corinthians 12:9a

We need to be content and stay joyful in our spiritual life, but there are times we need to push through for a breakthrough. You can work hand-in-hand with God to get into His timing for your life.

Most people back down too far, stop contending and just wait on God to open the door for them. If you have not seen the fulfillment of prophetic words over your life then you might be in a season in which you need to take steps of activation.

Ask, Seek And Knock: God's Timing

"Ask and it will be given to you; seek and you will find; knock and the door will be opened to you." Matthew 7:7

It is good to ask God for the timing of the prophetic word. Many times, it is for a season down the road. This is why understanding the Bible will help keep you on track. If you look at the examples in the Bible where people got a clear prophetic word, the next thing that happens is they go through the opposite of whatever the promise seemed to be.

A good example is when Samuel the Prophet anointed David to be the next king of Israel. This was the same type of anointing that Samuel had administered to the current King Saul. How mind-blowing that must have been for David! Samuel had already looked over all of David's older, taller, battle-tested brothers, but he summoned David from the fields for this amazing call on his life. David knew he would one day be king, but the rest of the family did not see it right away. (1 Samuel 16)

How David Activated His Prophetic Words

Although he knew the prophetic word was true (Samuel was revered as a prophet throughout Israel), David was forced into hiding and had to run from Saul's homicidal envy for years with a rag-tag group of misfits.

David needed that powerful word to hold onto because he was going to walk through the exact opposite circumstances before the promise would be fulfilled. God used all David's running and fighting the enemy to work His purposes into him.

David learned things on the run as a wanted man that he never would have learned sitting in a "school for kings and leaders." He learned honor, teamwork, putting others first, giant-killing, deliverance ministry (to King Saul), how to worship God in good times and bad, and the principle of not avenging yourself, but trusting God to take care of the matter. These are amazing character traits that served him well and won the hearts of the people over time.

Had he tried to rush the process, he may never have become the king, and do you think the people would have trusted a man who would kill a sitting king, even in self-defense? David passed his difficult tests and ascended when the time was right. David did not shrug and sit at home after Samuel's visit. He started his preparation by being a man after God's own heart, no matter what was happening to him. He activated the word Samuel gave him by being filled with the Holy Spirit and taking risks like coming against Goliath when others were afraid.

Moving Forward By Faith

You will see this principle with the apostle Paul as well. In Acts 9, Paul's name was originally Saul and he was on the road to Damascus, because he was persecuting Christians. He presided over the death of Stephen, the first martyr of the early Church. He was about to be called into a level of ministry like no one else had ever experienced, where he would be called to take the message of Jesus to the entire world.

When the stakes are that high you need a powerful prophetic word to carry you through the challenging times. God was pretty much calling him to change jobs and move. Not only that, but he had to change his name too! These are big decisions. Jesus appeared to Saul in a light that literally blinded him, and the voice from Heaven called him into his life purpose and destiny. But first he walked through the exact opposite of that.

He encountered the living Christ who confronted him with his ministry and methods. Saul immediately saw the error of his ways and repented. But the encounter left him physically blind, so God brought him to a Christian who prayed that he would have his sight back. Saul's reputation was so fierce that the man was afraid to let him in his home.

After being reassured by Saul's radical conversion, he prays and Saul, now renamed Paul, is miraculously healed. He then studies in obscurity for over a decade. He did not meet the original Apostles for years. He did not try to assert himself or take a place at the table with the other Apostles. He went through this incredibly difficult time. The Apostles were not sure if they could trust him at first. Learning to overcome rejection was part of his journey and it will be a part of yours as well. Just know this, when you get a powerful word, sometimes it is designed to get you to hold on through a hard storm. If you think about it, you do not need powerful words to do normal things. There are a lot of things in life that you do not need a powerful prophetic word in order to accomplish. Sometimes the greater the calling or the greater the prophetic word, the tougher the path is going to be, and the more resistance you are going to face. That is why God has given you that clarity. It is so that you will remember God's Word and not give up.

We All Have A High Calling

We are all born with a higher calling to make a difference in our lives and the world. Jeremiah 29:11 talks about God's desires for us to prosper and fulfill the plans He has for us all. But we can then drop down to a lower level of God's intentions for us. This happens as a result of what we believe about God and ourselves.

"... all things are possible to him who believes." Mark 9:23b NKJV

It is also influenced by warfare against us. This is the reason that God sends us prophetic words that seem higher than what we could ever do in our current situation. This is to stretch us and encourage us to go for all that He is calling us to. Big prophetic words spoken to us do not mean that these things will happen automatically. As I have been saying, we need to contend for it.

It is good to desire these higher callings, but remember to be faithful with the level that God has already given to you.

You will not be promoted to higher levels unless you are mastering your current sphere of influence that God has given to you. We all must go through this process of maturation.

I talk with a lot of people who want to have a well-known prophet call them up with a powerful prophetic word, have a visitation from an angel or from Jesus Himself to commission them and announce their calling. Most people who are seeking after these types of experiences will not get them.

If you are pursuing your calling and consistently doing the things that God has called you to do, then you do not need a blinding experience like Paul had. It is more about getting God's heart and love for people. Once you do that, then all of the other things fall into place. Do not forget what Paul said about prophecy.

"I keep asking that the God of our Lord Jesus Christ, the glorious Father, may give you the Spirit of wisdom and revelation, so that you may know him better." Ephesians 1:17

Having the spirit of wisdom and revelation has the purpose of knowing God better. As we put our focus on building our relationship with God while loving and encouraging others, then all the other things will indeed fall into place in our lives. We will undoubtedly understand God's will and timing for our lives much more clearly. In the next chapter I will discuss more about the higher levels of prophetic words, but let's keep in mind what their purpose actually is.

WHEN PROPHECY CARRIES MORE WEIGHT

As we just discussed in the previous chapter, there are some prophetic words that seem to carry more weight than others. We will need to take into consideration how to discern this. Some prophecy is designed to encourage you and other times it is a serious directional word. Some prophetic words are for a season down the road and some are a *now word* requiring an immediate response.

The prophetic words spoken over David and Saul (apostle Paul) were dramatic examples of prophetic words to call them to do something that would radically change the world. Remember that you do not need these types of encounters to do most of what God is calling you to do.

Some things to keep in mind for discerning this is how did the prophetic word come to you? Explaining spiritual things with words can be tricky, because we are expressing heavenly things in human terms. So these are simply metaphors or everyday examples to describe what are really more like processes, or experiences. Bearing that in mind, let's look at some of the different types of prophetic messages in terms of stages.

Levels Of Prophecy

When you are learning something, you start at a smaller, lower stage that is easy for you to understand. God starts us off easy to help us get comfortable. Although God does as He pleases, this is not a formula! As you learn to hear, you are hearing from this first stage. These prophetic words would tend to come as impressions, as opposed to a super clear message. They could be a word of knowledge that someone speaks out, or maybe a short simple dream, something along those lines.

Receiving prophetic words at this first stage does not mean it is inferior by any means. Everything from God is valuable! A prophetic word in this first stage just means that it is not something you want to move across the country on. It is not something you want to base any major decision or changes on. That is not to say that a prophetic word on this level is not encouraging. They can be life-changing! A first stage word could be, "God loves you," which perhaps does not sound all that powerful. But if you say that to a person who is down and out, and you say it at the right time, they may burst into tears and open their hearts to love. As a result, their life could be changed forever.

The next stage of a prophetic word or encounter might be something that comes in a greater form. Maybe the presence of God came over you so strong that you could not get off the floor.

Perhaps there was an angel that came to visit you, or you experienced the strong presence of the Holy Spirit through your five natural senses. You may have had a radical dream or vision that has stuck with you. These are important to note.

The next stage would include higher levels of experience that come within a dream. Maybe an angel comes in a dream and says, "This is everything you need right now." These are often powerful prophetic words and if this is what God is speaking, they actually can move you to a level of maturity. Higher-level encounters can include a visitation from an angel or even Jesus Himself. There can be words and experiences along those lines that would let you know you are experiencing a higher level of communication with God.

Having Spiritual Experiences

There is something important that I want you to know. Having experiences as I have described is not actually the purpose of the prophetic gifts. Sometimes we can get around prophetic communities, and we start wanting to have these higher-level experiences because we hear about them and we read the books by these people who have been taken into Heaven, for instance. I realize I am one of the prophetic ministers who share my supernatural encounters. I try to do it in a way that will draw you to the heart of God and to practically change your life.

For a number of years I operated in my prophetic ministry without having a dramatic encounter with God. An angel did not appear to my mother to announce my calling. I have never been in the Throne Room of Heaven, and until just a few years ago, I had never had an encounter with the Lord.

In 2002, when I started speaking and ministering with higher-level prophetic people, I have to admit that

I felt inferior at times. I heard the stories of all their supernatural encounters, and even though I was able to hear God clearly, I was not having these encounters. I have actually had to be content with operating at the level that God had me at, while at the same time learning to contend with and ask for more.

What I learned is that most people would not survive an encounter with the Lord. This is why in the Bible many people fell down as if they were dead when they had powerful spiritual encounters. It would take you out of commission for days and draw so much spiritual warfare against you that most people would not survive it. I am sure this is why God speaks to me in a different way, and I usually have prophetic dreams and encounters with angels (mostly unseen).

The point I am trying to make is that it is important to be humble and content with what you have now while you ask God for more. Do not make it your goal to get a powerful prophetic word or have a spiritual experience. Seek God's heart and character in your life, then all the other things will flow in at the right time. By the way, I did have an encounter with Jesus on August 31, 2014. He came into my home to tell me about the next phase of my life and spoke a powerful prophetic word to me. Do not envy this experience. This drew so much warfare and demonic attack against me that I got sick for two years and almost died. The resistance to higher callings and prophetic words can sometimes be intense but there is still a purpose for them.

Give And You Shall Receive

All prophetic words and experiences should point to Jesus. Here are a few scriptures to show that:

"For it is the Spirit of prophecy who bears testimony to Jesus." Revelation 19:10b

"… Anyone who has seen me has seen the Father … " John 14:9

" … the Son can do nothing by himself; he can do only what he sees his Father doing, because whatever the Father does the Son also does.." John 5:19b

They are all about coming closer to Him. It is not about an experience or anything like that.

That being said, there are times when you are desperate and need to hear God. There are some times when you need a prophetic word to get you through to the next season of your life. I have been there, and I know what it is like. It has filled me with compassion for people. I never want to forget what God has done for me, and what He can do for others.

That is why I give out a lot of prophetic words. I spent over ten years giving over 5,000 prophetic words a year at least. Now I am moving into a new season with my prophetic gifts in which I give less volume, but the words I do give are based in wisdom and understanding times and seasons.

This is a very powerful spiritual principle. I prophesy a lot because of the principle of giving and receiving. The more you give the more you receive. Some people think that these verses in the Bible about giving and receiving are just about money, but they are not. It is also referring to time, love, resources, the prophetic flow and all the gifts of the Spirit. This is how God set up His Kingdom. He has an endless supply of all we need, so we never have to be afraid to give away what He gives us. It flows back toward Him as worship and gratitude, and the flow is unending.

When I started to give a higher volume of prophetic words, it was because I needed direction in my life. So I started giving out the very thing that I needed, and guess what? The more you give, the more you receive. What you sow, you will reap. If you are sowing encouragement, goodness and direction to others then you will begin to reap these same things like never before. You will start hearing God more clearly because doing this will create an open Heaven over you.

If you start to practice sowing into the lives of others, you will find that you get unstuck in those areas of your life. That is what I mean by a breakthrough. You will begin to get breakthroughs because your sowing eventually catches up with you. If you have listened to my material, read my books, or heard me teach, you will hear me say this: most of the people who are not hearing God or getting a breakthrough are stuck because they are not sowing goodness, which is the fruit of the spirit. Or they are caught up in judgments that will close the Heavens over them.

Most people are sowing grumbling and complaining, and they are sometimes even calling it intercession, but in reality they are sowing the opposite of God's ways. If you want to see change in your life now, begin to sow goodness, love, joy, peace, patience, kindness, goodness, faithfulness, gentleness and self-control. This is the fruit of the Spirit. Also begin to sow love, gratitude and generosity. If you start to sow these things on a regular basis, it is going to catch up to you and overtake you. It is actually the secret to my success in the Kingdom. I just sow continually and you can do it too. If you keep sowing, then eventually you will become a sowing machine!

Change Of Seasons

Sometimes our season can change and things that worked in the older season will not be as effective in the new. The reason for this is that as we advance into higher levels of maturity, God will also advance our spiritual gifts. After years of doing what I call *rapid-fire prophecies* in which I would give hundreds of prophetic words to people at my live events, my prophetic gift began to change. I found that it was taking more effort and I would get exhausted doing the things I used to do with ease.

I am now operating in more of a *times and seasons* style of prophecy. God gives me insight and understanding into the season we are in and wisdom on how to operate in it. One of the reasons I wrote this book is to help people hear God's voice and activate it in their life. This is what God is calling us to do in the season we are in right now.

ACTIVATING A PROPHETIC WORD

God can speak to you through the Holy Spirit, other people, the Bible and so many different ways. I recommend recording these things and studying them. If you are wondering how to start and what to write down, ask yourself, "What is God saying to me right now?" Are there any confirming verses that come to mind? What are some practical steps that you can take to activate your words and impressions? Put that in the notes as well. Give yourself a couple of small steps that you can take. Consider giving yourself a deadline for completing them and write that down as well.

Pray and ask God to give you insight and make notes. Be sure to return to it now and then to see if you have more understanding than you did at first. Every time you add to it, be sure to record the date in a journal. You will need to keep track of these things because that is how you are able to discern what God is saying. You will see your understanding grow over time. You begin to have a history of hearing God and it gets easier.

How I Started

I have been hearing God in some form most all of my life. His voice started to become clearer in 1988. I had just come out of a terrible season in my life. I went through a rough divorce, was back on drugs and involved in the occult.

I had a dramatic encounter with Jesus and found myself back in church after seven years of being involved in deep darkness. I got counseling and was getting cleaned up, so to speak, and God began speaking to me more clearly.

Just a few months into my new spiritual journey, the presence of God came into my bedroom and spoke to me from Isaiah 61. That was the first time I heard a prophetic word for myself. To be honest, I did not even know if there was an Isaiah 61 in the Bible. I was shocked when I read it.

"The Spirit of the Sovereign Lord is on me, because the Lord has anointed me to proclaim good news to the poor. He has sent me to bind up the brokenhearted, to proclaim freedom for the captives and release from darkness for the prisoners." Isaiah 61:1

This bible verse hit me in my spirit and God's love enveloped me while I prayed. I cried for weeks after that experience. It was so powerful that I contacted my pastor and shared it at a home bible study. My friends around me were very skeptical that God would call me to preach considering that I had been on drugs just a few months before.

My church recommended that I get involved in various ministries and get grounded first. That was my first step to activate the prophetic words that God had spoken to me that day. But I hit more rocky times over the next three years of my life and found myself feeling far away from the powerful experience I had. In fact, I stopped going to church and started drinking again.

Then in 1991, God began moving in my life. It was like a light switched on and I could hear His voice more clearly and I started going to church again. It was that year that I received a prophetic word that would change my life forever.

I met a humble man named Pastor Hatfield who had a small meeting in his garage in Covina, California. He was such an accurate prophet and he is now in Heaven. I had been given prophetic words before, but never one with such depth and to this day all the things he spoke from God have come to pass.

He did not even know me, but he had me stand up and he told me that I was being called by God into ministry. He went into details of how I would be picking up on callings and giftings that other people would be letting go, and how I would be moving in dreams and visions (at the time I was not). He said that I would be traveling around the world and that I would be sought after, but first I needed to learn how to follow others and learn to serve.

Not only was it a powerful prophetic word, but the presence of God came very strongly to confirm it. He had never done this before to anyone he did not know, but he ordained me as a minister of the Gospel that night. People in my life, including those at my church, knew I had just come out of a backslidden condition. Really, it was a tough time. Some of my friends knew about it and were wondering why I was getting this powerful prophetic word and being ordained. They did not agree at all.

To activate this prophetic word I began volunteering at a homeless mission and visiting people in hospitals and nursing homes. I made myself available to whatever God wanted me to do; all the while I was working a fulltime corporate job in San Francisco. Within months, I preached my first sermon at a street mission and I began ministering to inmates on Death Row in San Quentin.

All of those powerful prophetic words did not come about right away, which makes sense to me now, in hindsight. At the time, I got excited and started looking for ways to activate the word. I did not start a ministry; instead I started serving everywhere I could. It often takes time for prophetic words to be worked out in your life. God will use the prophetic to get you on track, encourage you and help you to accelerate into your life's calling.

Isaiah 61 became and is still my life verse. It was seven years later that I was ordained as a pastor and we planted our first church in 1998. In 2011, I was commissioned as a prophet, though I had been operating as one for a number of years.

It sounds like I knew what I was doing and had a plan, but in reality it has been a rough time over the years and there has been a lot of adversity and difficult trials in my life that led me to do what I do now. But God will use these things to help us to grow and help others get through their tough times too.

Begin To Prepare Now

Trust God to speak to you and guide you, but do not forget to activate what He is saying to you. If you are called to do something that you are not released to do yet, or you are not at a mature enough level to do yet, then do not worry about that. You can still begin to prepare now. You can take a class, read a book or watch videos on the things you are called to do.

I knew I was called to public speaking but did not know where to start. So I volunteered to lead talks at work or in my church. I started studying the Bible much more seriously in 1991 after I got those life-changing prophetic words. I wanted to go to bible college, but I was in debt and still had all kinds of things going on in my life that I needed to work out.

I was going to twelve-step meetings and getting counseling. I had a job. I had child support to pay and other issues. But every morning, I would get up at 5:00 a.m. and I would go and pray at the church I attended. I would come home and make notes on what God was speaking to me. I would then go to my corporate job in San Francisco. At lunch, I would study the Bible, listen to teaching tapes and do study workbooks that I bought from the local Christian bookstore. This was before we had the Internet like we have now. My point is that you can be preparing for your future by doing things now.

Breakthrough Strategies

Today, we have so many resources including ministry schools and online training. Back then, we did not have these things, but we still had the Bible. So you can study, listen to audios, read books and take classes. This is how you activate the things that God is calling you to do. These are simple, easy-to-do action steps. The resources that God has right now are amazing. What can you do right now?

I mentioned this earlier, and it is worth repeating: if you want to learn to discern it is good to go back to the last time that God spoke to you clearly. Think about the details. How did it come to you? Did it come to you in a dream or a vision? Was it external or internal? Pause and really focus on it. Think about it. How did it feel? What characteristics were there? Did it feel positive or negative? These are the times that you knew that God spoke to you. Has God ever spoken this way before and what was the result? Write down what you recall.

What did it feel like to believe and have God confirm what He said with His peace, His Word and whatever else He used? What was the result of those times and what happened? What can you learn from those situations? How can you apply that experience and knowledge to the prophetic words you are learning to discern today? That is an amazing process that has helped a lot of people. I know it has helped me over the years to learn to discern.

Activation Steps You Can Take

When things are not changing in your life, here are some steps that you can take to hear God for a breakthrough. Begin to pray daily for yourself or your situation. Write down or journal what you are hearing God say. Take Communion each day or quiet yourself and spend time with God. Anoint yourself with oil or anoint your house with oil. Find a team of a couple of people who can pray with you daily if possible. I hear people complain to me all the time, "I am not around people who know how to pray for my needs." Hey, take whatever you can get!

"... If two of you on earth agree about anything they ask for, it will be done for them by my Father in heaven." Matthew 18:19b

Even if it is through a text, or an email, whatever you have to do, just do it. Ask God to show you what Satan does not want you to see about your situation and take notes. That is a powerful prayer. Respond to what you are hearing and contact other ministries or organizations that offer the types of ministry you need to get your breakthrough.

Get prayer everywhere it is offered. If you need radical breakthrough, then you will need to take radical steps and cut off generational ties. Even if you have already done it, do it again. Break any demonic assignments.

Try taking a drive about thirty-five miles away from your home or office. If things change and you can hear God or you feel better, then there is something locally around your house or in the area that needs to be dealt with. If you can hear more clearly, then there is something that is coming against you demonically, or an assignment in your community.

Do not worry; get someone to help you break it off through prayer. Break off witchcraft and word curses. There are ministries devoted to help with these types of issues. There are ministries like Sozo, Restoring the Foundations, Healing Rooms or Elijah House. There are so many options available for you. Do not let the enemy break you down; get a breakthrough instead.

Ask God to show you what to do physically because there might be some things you can do, like changes in your diet, more exercise, cleaning out your home environment, etc. Find books or audios or DVDs that will help you in any of these areas. This is being proactive.

CREATING DECLARATIONS

A very powerful way to activate your prophetic words is to create strategic declaration statements and prayers. There is power in making declarations and decrees over your life that will align you with God's Word.

"You will also declare a thing, And it will be established for you; So light will shine on your ways." Job 22:28 NKJV

Pray and search for Bible verses to find some things that affirm the prophetic word that you have over your life and begin to declare them.

I made a declaration prayer out of Philippians 4:19:

"And my God will meet all your needs according to the riches of his glory in Christ Jesus."

A powerful prayer and declaration to make this verse come alive is to pray, "I call in the Heavenly provision needed for me to live a healthy and spiritually rich life."

Make a list of verses that speak to you or that have powerful promises that you need. Then write out a short prayer or declaring statement in your own words that captures this promise. I have an entire page of declarations that I keep on my desk and I pray them all the time.

Another one of my declarations is from Isaiah 45:3a

"I will give you hidden treasures, riches stored in secret places ..."

I declare and I decree that God is giving me riches hidden and stored up in secret places. God is going to open those up. Thank you, God, for giving me these things, the rich, deep revelation that I can use to help other people.

You can get creative with doing declarations. You can also combine it with worship and sing them to God. It is a very powerful way to bring Heaven to Earth and cause you to rise above your situation.

Final Word

There is so much I can say about this subject. I wanted to give you the basics to get you started along the way of hearing God's voice and activating the prophetic words in your life. I do this as a lifestyle and have found it to be so enriching. The more you study how God speaks to you, the clearer His voice will become.

A powerful prayer I love to say comes from Ephesians 3 where the apostle Paul gives a blessing that is still applicable to our lives today.

"I pray that out of his glorious riches he may strengthen you with power through his Spirit in your inner being, so that Christ may dwell in your hearts through faith. And I pray that you, being rooted and established in love, may have power, together with all the Lord's holy people, to grasp how wide and long and high and deep is the love of Christ, and to know this love that surpasses knowledge—that you may be filled to the measure of all the fullness of God.

Now to him who is able to do immeasurably more than all we ask or imagine, according to his power that is at work within us, to him be glory in the church and in Christ Jesus throughout all generations, for ever and ever! Amen." Ephesians 3:16-21

And now my prayer for you:

Father, I thank you for each person reading this. God, I thank you that you are going to activate us on a new level. I pray for this activation where we can take a prophetic word and we are able to take small steps to bump us up to the next level.

Revelation 4:1b says, *"Come up here, and I will show you what must take place after this."*

God, I ask you to allow us to rise above our current situations, to come up higher and get out of everyday distractions so that we are no longer hindered by the entanglement of the enemy or other people. Father, I pray each person reading this would get a breakthrough. I pray that you would show them what Satan does not want them to see about their situations.

And Father, I pray that you would open our spiritual ears and eyes so that we can hear from you, and that we would begin to hear your voice speaking to us on a regular basis. God, I pray all this so that they (as it says in Ephesians 1:17) would know you better Lord, and for that purpose we pray these things in the name of Jesus, Amen.

I am honored to be a part of your life and to help you along the way. I would love to hear how this book has enriched your life.

Please stay in touch with me and my team on my social media pages and let us know what happens as a result of reading this book.

Facebook: TheDougAddison
Twitter: DougTAddison
Instagram: DougTAddison

Blessings,
Doug

Special Bonus Content

As a thank you for purchasing this book, we are including, as a special bonus, Doug's short e-book–*How to Hear God's Voice Clearly for Yourself.* Until now, this material has only been offered in digital format.

Please enjoy this special bonus content which includes some activation exercises at the end to help you along in your journey to Hearing God better.

HOW TO HEAR GOD'S VOICE CLEARLY FOR YOURSELF

DOUG ADDISON

TIPS TO HEARING GOD'S VOICE

Introduction

Have you wanted to hear God more clearly and consistently in your life? Have you ever heard God speak to you but nothing ever came of it? Maybe you are wondering if the things you are hearing spiritually are from yourself, God or other sources? Possibly you have never heard God speak to you at all?

The things I just mentioned are common questions I get. I have been hearing God most of my life though I did not know that there are things you can do to sharpen your abilities. I have been training people to hear the voice of God, understand their dreams at night and use them to discover important clues about their life calling.

I have interpreted tens of thousands of dreams and I give thousands of prophetic words a year. I am not trying to boast, I am just letting you know that if someone like me can do it, then so can you. Since I am a practical trainer I love to share the secrets or insights that I learned the hard way. My hope and prayer is that you will be able to save time and even pain through what I am going to share with you.

I wrote this book to help answer those questions and hopefully help you along your journey. Whether you are just starting out or a veteran at hearing God, even if you could learn one thing that might help you then reading this will be worth your while.

Sometimes God speaks more clearly, but most of the time it comes in the form of a small, quiet voice inside us that unless we train ourselves to listen to it, can be considered a coincidence.

Eyes to See

God speaks in so many ways, yet most people miss it. One thing that Jesus often taught through the parables is that in the Kingdom of God we must have *eyes that see* and *ears that hear.* (Matthew 13:16) He was talking about seeing and hearing spiritual things so that we may come to know His voice.

God truly is speaking all the time, but most people are either missing or not understanding what is being said to them.

I base everything I do on Ephesians 1:17, *"I keep asking that the God of our Lord Jesus Christ, the glorious Father, may give you the Spirit of wisdom and revelation, so that you may know him better."*

The sole purpose of hearing God and the reason I wrote this book is so that you may know Him better! The closer we get to God the clearer His voice becomes. Many people have stopped believing that God still speaks today. Learning to hear the voice of God is a lifelong process, but it is simple enough that even a child can do it.

No Limits at Hearing God

I want to invite you on a journey to hearing God daily in your life. You will never be the same. Because God created the Heavens and the Earth and He created us in His image it means that we are all very creative. You have access to everything you need through the Holy Spirit.

Daily Prophetic Words

I have been hearing God for a long time and I have been releasing written prophetic words since 2002. A few years ago God spoke to me to begin posting short, encouraging words from the Holy Spirit on various social media sites each day. I started on Twitter and Facebook and currently my daily prophetic words are going all around the world in over five languages that I am aware of.

I write what God shows me and call them Daily Prophetic Words. For the most part these prophetic words are what I would call confirming words. In other words, people have already sensed God speaking the same message to them before they read the encouraging word. So there is a sort of "echo" to the prophetic word where God will often repeat Himself by giving a similar prophetic word to various people to reassure them that they have heard Him accurately. It is not like these are weighty prophetic words.

Most are words of knowledge (you will find these explained in 1 Corinthians 12). These prophetic words are usually about the present or the past and some are a bit about the future. The Daily Prophetic Words are very short because I release them on Twitter and social media sites that have a limit in the number of characters you can use. I generally get them a month or more in advance, one for each day of the month.

They are not for every person on every day. But more times than not, God uses the Daily Prophetic Words to speak to people and give them encouragement. I am often surprised myself when I read them each day.

Prophetic Blogs and Articles

I also release weekly and monthly prophetic words through my Internet blog on my website DougAddison.com. These are actually much more prophetic in nature (that is, about the future as well as encouraging). God has gifted me to understand the times and seasons. So my weekly and monthly prophetic articles often contain specific dates and periods of times.

I basically report what God speaks to me about the specific season that we are in as a Church or people at large. Again, it might apply to every person but I get a lot of feedback that it is exactly what masses of people are experiencing.

I try to explain as much as I can about how these words came to me. I try to let people know that it is not always mystical to hear God. It actually becomes naturally supernatural when you grab hold of the ability to hear God on a daily basis. I try to demystify it and to really activate people into recognizing the fact that God is speaking all the time.

We Can All Hear God!

You do not have to be a prophet to hear the voice of God. In fact, this is a misunderstood aspect of how God speaks. Hearing God and prophetic ministry is meant to be a function in our lives and community. You may hear God differently than others because we are all uniquely created by God and have different gifts and styles.

"Now you are the body of Christ, and each one of you is a part of it." 1 Corinthians 12:27

Here are a few things I get asked most often about hearing God:

- How do I know if what I am hearing is from God or myself or the enemy?

- I am afraid of being deceived so how can I trust what I am hearing?

- I have stepped out before and responded to what God spoke to me but why was it that nothing happened?

- I often have dreams but how can I know which ones are from God?

In my training courses, books and blogs I answer these questions by helping people "learn to discern." When I say "learn" that means it takes practice and time to develop and mature. Just because God might speak to one person more clearly does not make them special or better. God loves us all the same.

Prophecy and revelation is given to us by God through the Holy Spirit and is intended to be a function in our lives and community. It is also intended to be encouraging to people who need a breath of life.

"But everyone who prophesies speaks to men for their strengthening, encouragement and comfort." 1 Corinthians 14:3

The Old Testament is full of examples of judgmental prophecies. But this was to get the

Israelites, God's people, back on track. That will not work with people who do not have a biblical foundation to begin with like we have today in our society. It was also done before people had the Holy Spirit in them like we do in the New Testament times.

I realize that not everyone who is reading this is all in the same place spiritually. I promise not to preach or tell you what to believe. I know that some of the things I am talking about might sound controversial or even stretch you at times but they are built on a biblical foundation and a lifetime of experience.

We can be *naturally supernatural* so to speak. Hearing God does not need to be spooky or mystical. I like to think of the supernatural things of God as being a *natural part of our lives*. You do not have to be a prophet to hear the voice of God.

God Longs to Speak to You

He longs to convey messages of love, comfort, guidance, and warning through a variety of different methods. Maybe it is through dreams and visions (Job 33:15–16), through the Bible (Daniel 9:2), through a conversation we have with someone, or through the arts like music, dance, paintings and sculpture. The possibilities are endless.

God longs for us to spend time with Him. Sometimes He gives us a puzzling dream just so we will search out the answer. And when we find the answer, it might seem insignificant, but God loves us so much that He is thrilled when we search for Him as we would for buried treasure. We can often miss God's still, gentle voice if we do not slow down enough to listen.

Hearing God in Daily Life

I had a dream that a friend of mine was crying. The next day I sent an email of encouragement and found out that he was going through a major crisis at work and my prayers really helped.

Wouldn't it be great to hear God tell you to take a different way to work, and as you did, you avoided a huge accident on the freeway? Or to hear God subtly nudge you to buy flowers for your spouse, and when you got home you found out that they had one of the worst days ever? How about hearing God tell you to go to the bank and withdraw a certain amount of money, and later that day you were in need of that exact amount of cash?

A while back my wife was driving in the fast lane of the freeway in fast moving bumper-to-bumper traffic in Los Angeles, and she heard the still small voice of God inside say, "back off", so she did. Instantly the car in front of her had a blow out and had she not backed off she would have crashed. These are some examples to illustrate that God wants to guide us every day in every way. These are ways God wants to interact with us regularly; however, to hear God consistently and accurately takes practice.

"But solid food is for the mature, who by constant use have trained themselves to distinguish good from evil." Hebrew 5:14

Many people are afraid of being deceived when it comes to hearing God. According to Hebrews 5:14, the remedy for this is to train yourself, which will take practice.

Secrets to Hearing God

Someone asked me what my secret is to hearing God? Is it fasting, prayer? What do I do? Well I practice, a lot! I record and write detailed things in a journal about how I hear God. I take notes and research what I am hearing and then I do it over and over.

Things like fasting, prayer, worshiping and reading the Bible develop the positive spiritual atmosphere we need to grow and mature. It keeps our heart and spirit sensitive to God's ways and keeps us from getting calloused. I like comparing these things to changing the oil in a car. It does not make it go faster, but instead it makes it last longer.

Different Ways God Speaks To Us

There are so many different ways that God can speak to us. I am going to cover just a few as a brief overview.

God Speaks Through the Bible

The most common way we hear the voice of God is through a verse in the Bible. Other times it is something that flashes through your mind. Not everything that we hear is necessarily from God. But practice will allow you to more easily discern what is and is not from God.

When you truly hear from God, it will never:

- violate principles from the Bible

- do anything that will harm others

- ask you to do something illegal

God Speaks Through Impressions or Pictures

Sometimes you may get something internally in the form of a picture in your mind or something quickly pops into your spirit. It may not necessarily be a complete thought but you sense it is from God ... be discerning, because not all of our thoughts are from God. It could come as a single word or phrase, or a song. You may suddenly see a picture of a rose. You then think about what it represents. A rose brings nice fragrance and beauty wherever it is.

There are also impressions from God that may come to you externally in the form of a vision or picture, or something externally that catches your eye. This could be repeated numbers on a clock, colors, or anything that God brings to your attention. For a split second you are drawn to the pen on the table, and God nudges you that writing is significant for you. Or you might remember that you wanted to write a thank-you note to a friend.

God Speaks Through Dreams and Visions

Dreams at night can be a great way to hear God. Though not all dreams are from God, once you understand how God speaks through symbolic language, then you can trust God to guide you.

Over one third of the Bible is made up of dreams and visions. Jesus often spoke in parables, and dreams are very similar to *night parables.*

"For God may speak in one way, or in another, yet man does not perceive it. In a dream, in a vision of the night, when deep sleep falls upon men, while slumbering on their beds, Then He opens the ears of men, and seals their instruction. In order to turn man from his deed, and conceal pride from man." Job 33:14-17 NKJV

Other Ways That God Speaks to Us

There are many ways that God can speak to us, but I do not have the time in this book to go into all the details. Jesus said more than fifteen times that we must have *eyes that see and ears that hear.*

He was referring to seeing and hearing spiritually. Jesus taught powerful principles about the Kingdom of God by using parables.

These symbolic stories from real life situations conveyed a deeper spiritual truth. Even Jesus' disciples who were close to Him did not understand this way of communication at first (Matthew 13). You can learn a lot about God's hidden language by studying Jesus' parables and how He described their meanings to the disciples.

God may speak to us through other people. What may seem like a normal conversation with a friend could be God trying to communicate something to you. Remember, God can speak through movies, music and the arts.

God often speaks through nature or natural things. Take a walk in the woods and allow creation to speak to you through its beauty and splendor. Often things that happen in the natural realm are reflective of what is happening in the supernatural.

There are other ways to hear God, which may include things like supernatural experiences, angels, and hearing an audible voice from Heaven. These are all very biblical, and though they are not as common, they cannot be ruled out as a means to hearing God.

Keep in mind that you do not need a dramatic encounter or to hear the audible voice of God. Most people are waiting for an angel to show up or a major sign from Heaven to drop in front of them.

God is speaking to you daily and longs for you to pay attention to the small nudges He is already giving you.

God Does Not Despise Immaturity

God sees you as who you are becoming even though you will still need to go through a process of development. God is not impatient with immaturity and enjoys relating to you as you grow. You would never expect a five-year-old child to drive a car.

In the same way God does not expect more from us than our current level of maturity allows. As you grow and mature, God will test you for the purposes of promoting you into a greater level of influence and maturity.

GOD SPOKE, NOW WHAT?

Five Steps to Hearing God Daily

As I share these tips to hear God daily it is so important to not become legalistic about doing them. There is not a formula to follow and you are not a bad person for not doing some of these things daily. There is so much freedom in our spiritual life and we are no longer bound by rules and regulations. These are just guidelines that you can use.

1. Believe: There is a lot of power that happens when we believe.

"But when you ask, you must believe and not doubt, because the one who doubts is like a wave of the sea, blown and tossed by the wind." James 1:6

Most people believe that God still speaks today, just not necessarily to them. And if we continually focus on not being able to do something, chances are we never will. But if we change our focus and accept that God loves us and longs to speak to us, there is a good chance we will begin to hear God in ways we never thought possible.

There is a spiritual principle that unbelief chokes out supernatural experiences from God. An example of this is found in Matthew 13:58, when Jesus was not able to do many miracles due to the unbelief of the people. God really does desire to communicate with us. Most of the time, we simply need to clear away some of the busyness in our lives to perceive what He is saying.

Believing activates our faith. It is necessary to develop an atmosphere of faith in order to open up the spiritual principles necessary to mature in hearing God daily. We all are driven by our belief systems whether negative or positive, known or unknown. Most of our beliefs were formed in us at a young age. It is necessary at some point in your life to evaluate your beliefs and look for ones that may be hindering you from hearing God more clearly.

2. Make sure you are at peace.

"But Jesus often withdrew to lonely places and prayed." Luke 5:16

We must have peace in our lives if we want to hear the voice of God daily. When we are hurried or stressed out, we are less likely to consistently hear Him. Many people hear God when they are in the shower or taking a bath.

This may seem surprising, but it is because it is one of the few places where we are alone and able to listen.

It is good to set time aside regularly, daily if possible, to quiet yourself. For me, the best time is first thing in the morning. I know we are all wired differently, but morning seems to be a good time because the phone is not ringing, there are fewer distractions, and things are the quietest. If you have small children, then maybe this is best later at night or in the afternoon.

Each morning I spend a few moments getting focused on God. For me, this includes praying, reading the Bible, and asking God to speak to me about my day. I write down the dreams I had at night and take notes and do some research on things I am hearing God speak to me.

Maybe you feel that you do not have time to do this, so do what you can. It would be nice if we all had quality time with God. But the truth is spending any time you have will be beneficial.

When I was a business owner in San Francisco I used to pull my car over on the way to work each day for 10–15 minutes to do what I am saying here. I also went out at lunch for prayer walks or to listen to the Bible on audio. You can combine two things to save time. I like to use the exercise-prayer combination so that my body, soul, and spirit are all working together.

God will often speak to us by impressing a verse on our minds. Reading the Bible regularly will help condition us to be more spiritually sensitive.

Sometimes God speaks to us clearly, and other times He is not as clear. God often conceals matters and requires those who really want more of Him to search for God as they would to uncover hidden treasure. If we spend time with Him, we will access the treasures of kings!

"It is the glory of God to conceal a matter; to search out a matter is the glory of kings." Proverbs 25:2

3. Remove hindrances to hearing God.

"Therefore, since we are surrounded by such a great cloud of witnesses, let us throw off everything that hinders." Hebrews 12:1

There will always be hindrances to hearing God daily. A major hindrance to hearing God can be our own theology. If we were taught that God does not speak today, then this will affect our ability to hear Him. Our traditions or forms of worship can also be a hindrance to hearing God because they often limit when and how God can speak.

When I first began to grow in my ability to hear God, I thought I had to be in a worship service to hear Him. I really do not know why, but I believed that if God was going to speak to me, it would probably be at church. The drawback to my way of thinking was that I was only in church once or twice a week, and the church I went to at the time had a quick, visitor-friendly type of service that did not allow much time to be quiet and listen to God.

Later, I realized that God is speaking all the time. There is no one way or method for hearing God. He is multi-faceted, and when we try to put Him in a box, we will miss the unlimited power and creativity available to us. It is a good idea to start noticing the ways God tends to speak to you. As you put your attention to it then you can grow and develop more.

A third hindrance to hearing God is being too busy to listen. Sometimes we can fill our time with activities that appear worthwhile but actually hinder us from hearing God daily. I have developed the ability to have the *eyes to see and ears that hear* that Jesus spoke so much about. There are hidden prophetic messages in movies, TV shows, commercials and music. So even if you watch TV or surf the internet you can tune in to the *Holy Spirit Network* and ask God to speak to you.

A fourth hindrance to hearing God is to assume we know what He is saying. This is called assumption or presumption. Often God speaks to us to reveal barriers and blocks in our relationship with Him. Our own beliefs, ego and pride can block the real meaning of what God is trying to show us. We may think He is speaking about something or someone else and not about our own issues. When we hear from God we need to first look at our own lives before we attempt to try to help someone else.

4. Activate what God is saying.

"But the one who hears my words and does not put them into practice is like a man who built a house on the ground without a foundation." Luke 6:49a

As God begins to speak to you, it is a good idea to value what you are hearing and write it down. Your life purpose and destiny depends upon these fundamental daily practices. It will help to get a notebook, a prayer journal, or type what you hear God saying in your computer in ways that best fits your personality and style.

Get into the habit of writing down what you sense God telling you. This will help you keep track of them. Give thanks to God when you see them happening, because it helps your spirit to focus positively on God's good nature.

If we want to hear God consistently, we must be quick and develop the habit of responding every time He speaks. Sometimes God will remain silent until we do the last thing He told us to do. Stop for a minute and ask God to show you whether there is anything you need to respond to.

Hearing God is so awesome and it is amazing that He wants to speak to us. A major key to hearing God daily is to activate or respond to the things that God speaks to us.

Jesus said, *"Ask and it will be given to you; seek and you will find; knock and the door will be opened to you."* Matthew 7:7

Notice that the words ask, seek and knock are all proactive steps. They also are an acronym: ASK. Jesus did not say, *Believe and the door will be opened.* Or even, *Sit on the couch and wait for God to open the door.* Again, there is power in believing and power in waiting on God. There is also power in taking action.

In order for you to grow in your ability to hear God and to find and fulfill the destiny God has for you it requires you to take steps and be proactive. There are many other similar principles in the Bible that are keys that will unlock and open the door to your future. They will also close doors to negative things from your past.

The problem is that most people only believe these principles in their minds and have not practiced them consistently in their daily lives. When we do them we will start to see the radical transformation of a new life.

You can activate things that you hear from God by taking some small practical steps that makes it come alive in your life. Things like writing it down, doing internet research, reading a book on the subject, sending an apology, praying, downloading an application, or starting to save money towards it. The list is endless. There is power in doing small things.

If you have been around my training long you will hear me talk about developing a Breakthrough Lifestyle. This is doing small things over time toward the things that you feel called to or that God speaks to you. If you make a habit of this, then you will create an atmosphere of breakthrough and not avoidance. This is the cure to procrastination, unclear vision or feelings of being stuck.

5. Practice.

"But solid food is for the mature, who by constant use have trained themselves to distinguish good from evil." Hebrews 5:14

For those who need them, you can actually put on your Holy Spirit training wheels. It is okay to practice. It is okay to make mistakes because that is the only way to learn. Find a safe place to practice. If you do not have a lot of experience, you may not want to start by sharing something in front of a group. Try with people who you know and let them know you are practicing.

I have trained a lot of people to use the line, "I am taking a class on hearing

God or how to encourage people ... can I practice on you?" Just know that God loves you, has grace for you and wants to use you. He wants to speak to you and you can trust the process.

Many people are afraid of being deceived when it comes to hearing God's voice. The remedy for this is to train yourself to distinguish between good and evil. This can only be done through practice. When I first started practicing hearing God, it freaked out people at my church. They told me I should not be doing that because it was like fortune telling.

Seriously?

God wants us to learn to hear His voice. Fortune telling is done through a different spirit than the Holy Spirit. Also, we permit people to practice all the other gifts mentioned in the Bible such as, teaching, administration, hospitality, etc.

Why not the prophetic? This is a blind spot for many people today and we would all benefit from having the freedom to *learn to discern* in a safe place.

Study the Real

We must learn to be sensitive to the differences between God's voice, our own ideas, and those of demonic forces. The easiest way to do this is to study your own experiences of how God has spoken to you in the past. Let's say you hear God and there is clear evidence to confirm that what you heard was really God speaking to you. Use a journal to record and study what it felt like to hear Him. Remember how it came to you, the sense you had in your spirit, and the peace you had.

So, how can we practice hearing God?

- First, ask God to begin to train you.

- Ask the Holy Spirit to make you sensitive to His voice.

- Write down what you feel God is speaking to you.

- Track your experiences and make notes on things you heard in advance that actually happened.

We are not trying to predict anything or be a prophet; we are simply asking God to speak to us so we can learn. It takes time and practice to recognize the difference between our own thoughts and words from God.

Focus On God and Not Demons

I mentioned grabbing hold of the authentic so that you will recognize the counterfeit. Unfortunately, some people today are actually too focused on the counterfeit. They are more focused on demons than they are on angels or the Holy Spirit.

How do I know this? Because I have had encounters with angels and when I start talking about it at a church or in a meeting people get uncomfortable. The odd thing is if I said, "I think there is a demon in the room," then probably 95% of these people would say, "Yes, I agree." This is a sad day when discerning demons is actually a higher value than discerning what the Holy Spirit or angels are doing in the room and that is where we need to flip this around.

Flipping a Negative Word

Whenever you see the destruction of Satan in a person's life you have the opportunity to speak God's will, not Satan's. Most negative words of knowledge and prophecy come from you discerning Satan's will for the person instead of God's. People who have a high destiny or calling on their lives will have more resistance and warfare. The good news for you is why would the enemy work so hard on you unless you were a threat.

There is power in being able to discern the plans of the enemy. But most of us have not been adequately training on how to respond to what we are seeing. Usually, God's will is the opposite—so "Flip it! And flip it good!" When you can learn to do this you will have an amazing power to stop the works of darkness.

Closing

Well, I have given you a lot in this book. I go deeper into all these principles in my training courses, books and blogs on my website. I encourage you to attend an online training event or take one of my in-depth training courses or coaching groups. I guarantee you that your life will never be the same! At the end of this book you will find three exercises that will help activate you in hearing God daily.

"I pray that the eyes of your heart may be enlightened in order that you may know the hope to which he has called you, the riches of his glorious inheritance in his holy people." Ephesians 1:18

Blessings,
DOUG ADDISON

EXERCISE: HEARING GOD

Here are a few exercises to hear God more clearly. Do not be discouraged if you are not able to hear Him clearly on any or all of these. It is a process.

1. *Hearing God through the Bible:* Ask God to give you a verse in the Bible that will speak to you personally. Close your eyes and do not think hard; just wait until something comes into your mind. This may take a few tries to get something practical.

2. *Hearing God through writing:* Take a piece of paper or use your computer, and begin to write what you feel God is speaking to you. Think of it as a love letter from your Father. Let it flow from deep inside you. Again it should be positive and uplifting and will not condemn you. God loves you and wants you to succeed.

3. *Hearing God through an object:* Pick up an object that is near you right now. Hold it in your hand and ask God to speak to you about yourself based on this object. Look at all sides of the

object, read it, and think symbolically. Write down what He tells you.

Want To Go Deeper?

If you enjoyed this material and these activation exercises, then you can find a lot more in-depth study and weekly activation exercises in the *Hearing the Voice of God 365 online activation school.* For more details, visit: HearingGod365.com

ABOUT DOUG

Doug Addison is a prophetic speaker, author, life coach and stand-up comedian. He is known for his *Daily Prophetic Words*, *Spirit Connection* webcast, podcast and blog. Doug's message of love, hope and having fun reaches people around the world! His unique style of teaching and coaching helps open people to discover their destiny and experience God's supernatural love and power. He and his wife Linda live in Los Angeles, California.

DougAddison.com

MORE RESOURCES FROM DOUG ADDISON

Hearing the Voice of God 365

Hearing the Voice of God 365 is an online prophetic activation school that comes to you! Through the twelve modules in this school, you will learn to discern the voice of God every day, grow in your gifts, walk in your identity and discover the destiny God has for you!

Hearing the Voice of God 365 is filled with how-to instruction by Doug, along with exclusive mentoring sessions with prophetic leaders including Lance Wallnau, Lana Vawser, Sandi Krakowski, and more. It also provides activation exercises designed to help you learn to hear the voice of God, deepen your relationship with Him and save you time! Learn more at: *HearingGod365.com*

How to Flip Your Financial Future

This book packs a powerful punch to activate you in practical kingdom strategies for sowing and reaping, getting out of debt, increasing your income, and even starting or growing your business or ministry, so you can *flip* your financial future ... and flip it good!

Understand Your Dreams Now: Spiritual Dream Interpretation

Doug Addison's *Understand Your Dreams Now: Spiritual Dream Interpretation* is drawn from decades of classroom and real-world experiences. It contains everything you need to get started or to go to a new level of interpreting dreams. Includes a 300-symbol dream dictionary.

Personal Development God's Way

People everywhere want to know their life's purpose and destiny. *Personal Development God's Way* was developed after Doug Addison spent a lifetime studying why some people's lives change radically and others do not. Packed full of practical examples, stories and exercises designed to apply to your life.

Accelerating into Your Life's Purpose

Discover your destiny, awaken passion and transform your life with this ten-day interactive program. Designed to reveal your life's desires, remove obstacles and create a written plan for what to focus on next. This program will help you change limiting beliefs, stop the past from affecting your future and develop a strategy to guide you towards your destiny. Includes ten audios and transformation journal.

Spiritual Identity Theft Exposed

The rise of identity theft in the world today parallels what is happening spiritually to people everywhere.

People have been blinded to their true identity and the destiny they were created to live. *Spiritual Identify Theft Exposed* contains seven strategies from darkness and seven remedies to change your life forever.

Write a Book Quickly: Unlock your Creative Spirit

Whether you are just starting out or are an experienced writer, this precise book can help you get to a new level. Tap into your creative nature, learn secrets of writing, publishing tips, writing resources, exercises, and more.

Dream Crash Course Online Training

Understanding dreams does not have to be difficult! Doug Addison is an expert dream interpreter who has interpreted over 25,000 dreams and has trained thousands of dream interpreters worldwide.

He has developed a *crash course* on how to understand your dreams quickly. This is everything you need in one online program. Includes ten online videos, MP3s, study guide, dream journal, symbols dictionary and more!

Prophetic Tattoo and Piercing Interpretation Online Training

Now you can learn the inside secrets to *Prophetic Tattoo and Piercing Interpretation* from Doug Addison. After years of development, Doug Addison is making this one-of-a-kind online training available to you. Find what you need to get started in this new cutting-edge outreach strategy! This online training includes seven online videos, MP3s, study guide, tattoo reference cards and more.

Activate Your Life Calling Online Community

Are you ready to bring lasting change in your life, now? Do you want to discover and fulfill your higher calling? Do you want passion to get up each day knowing you are working towards your purpose? Join us during this three-month interactive program to *Activate Your Life Calling*. This online coaching group is designed to bring the transformation in your life that you have always desired, whether that is helping you lose weight, getting a better job, launching a business or ministry, writing a book, or deepening your relationship with God ... we provide all the support, practice, and feedback you need to break through quickly! *Activate Your Life Calling* will give you all the tools you need to succeed!

Visit: dougaddison.com/store